NARROW GAUGE
RAILWAYS

ENGLAND AND THE FIFTEEN INCH

Narrow Gauge
RAILWAYS
ENGLAND AND THE FIFTEEN INCH

Humphrey Household

PRC

First published 1989 by Alan Sutton Publishing

ISBN 1 85648 178 6

This edition published 1995 by
The Promotional Reprint Company Limited,
exclusively for Bookmart Limited,
Desford Road, Enderby, Leicester LE9 5AD

Produced by Mandarin Offset
Printed and bound in China

To
RONALD and LILIAN
dear friends for many years
whose interest has given
great pleasure
and
encouragement

CONTENTS

—◁▷—

INTRODUCTION

What! More narrow gauge railways? Well, three of those I have written about, all in Yorkshire, have long since ceased to exist and were never well known, so a description of each, illustrated by the photographs I took in the 1920s, supplemented by some from other sources, may be of interest. The memory of another abandoned line, the Lynton & Barnstaple, has of course been preserved in print and by television programmes, but as some of the photographs I took of it in 1927 have not been previously reproduced, it seems reasonable to make such an attractive railway the subject of another chapter.

Much of the book is concerned with the 15-inch gauge railways pioneered in the last quarter of the nineteenth century by Sir Arthur Heywood of Duffield Bank, Derbyshire, who considered it the minimum gauge for effective carriage of passengers and freight. It was, he believed, particularly suitable for light railways to transport agricultural produce from farms on large estates and to meet military needs in time of war. Although, in fact, a wider gauge of 18in. or 24in. came to be preferred for both purposes, his 15-inch became popular for private garden railways and also on exhibition sites where the public could enjoy rides in trains of open carriages drawn by the scale model locomotives developed by the engineer Henry Greenly and the enthusiastic manufacturer of models, W.J. Bassett-Lowke. It is also, of course, the gauge of two popular tourist railways very much alive today: the Ravenglass & Eskdale amid the glorious scenery of the Cumbrian mountains and dales on the western flank of the Lake District; and the Romney Hythe & Dymchurch, a line designed and equipped as the perfect example of a large scale model railway and built across that strange flat, yet appealing, area known as Romney Marsh, a rich grazing and agricultural land dotted with isolated farmhouses, attractive villages and notable ancient churches.

As with the Lynton & Barnstaple, several books have been written describing in detail the two last-mentioned railways, but even so there may be a place for what may be described as an essay covering their inception, history and equipment, especially as I have covered recent developments in signalling and train control on each; operating methods have always interested me quite as much as locomotives and rolling stock.

I am much indebted for information, suggestions and pictures provided by Douglas Ferriera, General Manager, and Peter van Zeller, Archivist, Museum Curator and driver, of the Eskdale; John Snell, Managing Director, and George Barlow, driver for thirty years and Operating Manager for four years, of the Romney; and Neil Mackay who knew Harrogate well in his earlier days and sent me valuable information about the Gas Works Railway, including a photostat of the longitudinal section from the deposited plan which resolves once and for all the controversy concerning the gradients within that railway's tunnel. Valuable help has also been given me by D.H. Townsley, General Sales Manager of the Hunslet Engine Company; R.N. Redman of the Narrow Gauge Railway Society; and, in the distant past, Robert Hudson Limited, Light Railway Specialists. None can be blamed for errors which may remain.

My thanks are also due to John Slater, Editor of *The Railway Magazine*, for the use of maps; to the staff of Ashford Public Library for access to material in their remarkable Railway Room; and to the Guildhall Camera Centre, Folkestone, for photographic work. Above all, to Peter Clifford of Alan Sutton Publishing Limited to whom I owe much and with whom, during five years of association, a happy personal relationship has developed, tempered in the heat of occasional controversy!

I have acknowledged individually in the captions the sources of all illustrations reproduced, except those from my own photographs.

Humphrey Household
Folkestone, February 1989

CHAPTER ONE

MINIMUM GAUGE RAILWAYS FOR PUBLIC USE

W hat was the narrowest gauge on which public transport of goods and passengers was commercially possible? There had been doubt whether two feet was wide enough for successful operation of steam-hauled passenger trains until the Festiniog Railway proved that it was. Was this the limit? Sir Arthur Heywood, author of *Minimum Gauge Railways*,* thought not and experimented to prove the point on the estate at Duffield Bank, some four miles north of Derby, where he settled in 1872. He had long taken a keen interest in railways, and at the age of eighteen had built a 4-inch gauge locomotive and some wagons using the tools in his father's workshop. His serious experiments, however, began at Duffield Bank in 1874 and, because he found that the very narrow gauge materials then available commercially were 'mere toy imitations of those of the standard gauge' and quite unsuitable for useful transport, he decided to make everything himself on a robust scale capable of sustaining hard use, obtaining only rails, boilers and engine frame-plates from elsewhere. Although he claimed to be no more than 'a self-taught mechanic and surveyor', he developed such skill that he was quite capable of acting as draughtsman, moulder, machinist and fitter in his well-equipped workshops, where he employed seven or eight artisans whom he had trained.

He had built a 9-inch gauge railway which had delighted his younger

* Heywood, A.P., *Minimum Gauge Railways*. Privately printed 1881, 1894 and 1898; typewritten reproduction of text produced by C.R. Clinker, 1950.

Sir Arthur Heywood's 15-inch gauge Duffield Bank Railway doubles back on itself with sharp curves and stiff gradients to reach the 'main line' at the old quarries. (*David & Charles: Locomotive & General Railway Photographs Collection.*)

brothers, but experience had shown that the vehicles were not stable enough unless the passengers kept to their seats and 'did not attempt to ride on the ends and edges of the carriages and wagons' – which presumably his brothers had done! So the railway he began to install at Duffield Bank in 1874 was of 15-inch gauge. Starting with a line leading from the drive to the workshops near the house, this grew during the next seven years to a length of a little over a mile, including sidings, and was designed to test thoroughly the potential of the gauge. The extension from the workshops climbed for about a quarter of a mile on gradients of 1 in 10 and 1 in 12 as it rounded a severe curve and doubled back on itself to reach old quarries 80ft. higher, where there was space to lay a 'main line' with a loop at each end, part of it level, part on a gradient no worse than 1 in 20. Here there were three tunnels, two bridges, a timber trestle viaduct 19ft. long and 20ft. high, and six stations. The line was equipped with interlocking points and signals which were worked from two signal boxes linked by telephone.

Sir Arthur experimented with rails weighing from 12lb. to 22lb. per yard before settling on 16lb. as adequate. These were properly fish-plated at the joints and spiked to timber sleepers, which he later increased in thickness, width and length by about a quarter, but as the life of these was only some six years, he took to casting iron sleepers complete with chairs, or 'jaws', in which the rails were secured by spring keys.

As for the locomotives, he insisted that their total weight should be available for adhesion and that the overhang at the two ends should be equal. He therefore adopted a launch-type boiler, having a cylindrical firebox which could be fitted above the rear axle, unlike a normal locomotive firebox dropped between the frames behind that axle. There was, of course, some loss of heating surface, and in fact the launch boiler proved to be the least satisfactory feature of his design. He began with the four-coupled *Effie* but, seeking a locomotive capable of developing greater power and speed, he lengthened the chassis to carry a longer boiler, building the six-coupled *Ella* in 1881 and the eight-coupled *Muriel* thirteen years later. These, and three others built subsequently, had a certain amount of standardisation in design and construction, and were so sturdily built that four of the six lasted thirty years or more, and one, rebuilt with a locomotive boiler and other modifications, survives in service today, ninety-four years later.

The coupled wheels were small, varying in diameter from 13½in. to 18in., but nevertheless one engine achieved a speed of 23 mph on test, and the average speed in passenger service was about 11 mph. Each footplate had a front sheet with spectacles, but none had a cab, Heywood stressing that any cab would be inconveniently small, dangerous in emergency, uncomfortably hot in summer, and that for protection in inclement weather 'a stout mackintosh is cheaper and far better for the driver'! He built the first engine for £309, but estimated that a commercial price would have been nearer £400.

Passenger carriages were equally strongly constructed and long-lasting. Heywood mentioned seven bogie cars, all built on a standard frame, 19½ft. long and 42in. wide. Four, each weighing 1 ton, were open and seated sixteen persons, two abreast. One was enclosed and 4 cwt heavier. The other two were a remarkable demonstration of what could be achieved on such a narrow gauge, for one was a dining car with seating for eight and a cooking stove in a separate compartment, and the other, a sleeping car with four berths and a lavatory. There were other vehicles four-wheeled, such as a brake van, workmen's carriage, service vehicles and a number of small flat wagons on which could be placed box frames, two or three mounted on top of each other to increase capacity if needed, or bolsters so that a pair could carry long loads such as timber.

Sir Arthur's children of course loved running the railway – what fun it must have been to prepare and eat a meal in the dining car! And when Sunday School parties were invited, as they were periodically, excited members were thrilled by the rides they were given. Besides giving pleasure, the railway was useful in carrying timber and disposing of rubbish on the estate. But Heywood had much deeper and more serious uses in mind: to prove how economical a light railway could be in farm and estate management instead of horse-drawn cartage; and to provide the Royal Engineers with a system of transport they were looking for, a railway that could be quickly laid and easily moved within forward areas in time of war: hence the steep gradients, sharp curves, timber trestle viaduct, tunnels, and the dining and sleeping cars which might serve as mobile staff quarters.

However, in spite of the interest shown by RE officers, military use was not then developed; the high command was, and long remained, convinced that any future war would be one of such rapid movement that not even the easily-laid tracks of a narrow gauge light railway would enable railheads to be advanced quickly enough.

The prospect of use in estate management was more promising. From time to time, Sir Arthur held open days at Duffield Bank, and these were not confined to the Sunday School parties or to the more sedate garden parties in his grounds. In 1881, when the Royal Agricultural Society's show was held in Derby, the members were invited to inspect the railway and watch demonstrations staged to show how valuable one could be on a large farm; and when another exhibition was held in 1894, primarily for engineers, one of the visitors was the Hon. Cecil Parker, agent to the Duke of Westminster at Eaton Hall, near Chester, where transport to and from the nearest railway station was a major problem. Balderton, on the GWR Shrewsbury–Chester main line, was three miles away, and from there about 6,000 tons of coal, road metal, building materials and general merchandise were being carried annually by horse and cart, besides which there was a certain amount of outward traffic in timber, bricks and pipes from the estate sawmill and brickworks. Parker had been drawn to the exhibition by the thought that a light railway might well be more economical, and Sir Arthur soon convinced him that at Eaton Hall they had 'a perfect opportunity for a practical experiment with the 15in. gauge', which could readily carry 'five times that amount' of traffic.

Parker put the suggestion to the Duke, who approved, provided the line was unobtrusive, especially where it could be seen from the Hall. Heywood was asked to inspect the site and make a rough estimate of the cost. This, he considered, would be about £6,000, exclusive of any necessary buildings.

But who was to build it? After some doubt as to whether he could spare the time, he decided that he himself would have to survey, construct and equip the railway, because no commercial firm had sufficient experience in manufacturing such small scale, yet robust, material, nor had any contractor knowledge of laying such narrow track, nor dare navvies be trusted to work where game was preserved!

So Heywood himself 'worked away . . . with beater, rammer and crowbar', while his assistant engineer learnt his ways and his sixteen men were trained. Although the maximum gradient against the load was restricted to 1 in 70, earthworks were light. The formation was carefully prepared, and the track, laid with steel rails on iron sleepers, was well ballasted with cinder which, through the park, was rendered as inconspicuous as possible by sinking it level with the turf. Level crossings at three principal drives and the main road to Wrexham were formed so as not to inconvenience passing vehicles. Intersections of field boundaries were made secure by digging pits and carrying the rails across on girders too narrow to afford lodging for the feet of cattle. Girder bridges crossed several brooks.

Including a branch line to the estate works and sidings to the electricity generating plant and elsewhere, the length of the railway was 4½ miles. Track-laying began in August 1895, reached the Hall by Christmas, and by May 1896 was all but complete on the branches. To work the line, Heywood supplied an 0–4–0 named *Katie*, thirty four-wheeled wagons of 22 cwt. capacity, six to carry 1½ tons and two to take 2 tons, a brake van, and two bogie vehicles, one of which was a passenger coach, the other a parcels van. All this he provided at cost price, without charge for his own time, and for just over £100 *less* than his estimate, an achievement rarely equalled by a contractor before or since. The buildings, coal store, engine shed, carriage and wagon sheds, were designed by him but built by estate staff to 'a high, and probably expensive, standard'.

Curiously, *Katie* proved to be the least reliable of Heywood's engines and, as a substitute had to be borrowed from Duffield Bank from time to time, two 0–6–0s were later supplied to Eaton Hall. After the First World War a Simplex petrol locomotive was acquired, probably from the War Surplus Disposals Board, and the steam engines became little used, especially after an improved Simplex was obtained in 1938.

The Eaton Hall railway fulfilled all expectations, carrying freight for threepence per ton-mile less than road cartage. It remained in service for just over fifty years until 1947, when it was disposed of lock, stock and barrel, to the Romney Hythe & Dymchurch Railway. And there, at New Romney, Heywood's sturdy but primitive little brake tender is preserved in working

Eaton Hall Railway goods brake tender at New Romney in April 1988.

Comparison in size of 15-inch gauge locomotives: the little Cagney engine, bought by Charles Bartholomew in 1903 for his Blakesley Hall Railway, was restored to working order about 1960 and is shown here in 1969 alongside the Romney Hythe & Dymchurch Railway Pacific No. 10. (*George Barlow.*)

order, though unable to be used because its height exceeds the Romney loading gauge.

Sir Arthur Heywood had certainly proved the capability of the 15-inch gauge. He had sown the seed in 1874, and tended the plant at Duffield Bank and Eaton Hall. Forty years later, hybrids grew and flourished at Eskdale in Cumberland and Fairbourne in Merionethshire, and later still at Romney in Kent. But a true scion from the stock took root near York in the early 1920s when a narrow gauge railway was built expressly to serve the farms on the Sand Hutton estate. There it blossomed for a while before it withered and finally died, blighted by the growth of a more adaptable species.

★   ★   ★

Around the turn of the century, enthusiasm for railways was near its height, and old and young who had the means acquired small steam locomotives they could run on tracks in house or garden. Furthermore, those who were less well-heeled seized whatever opportunity came their way to ride as fare-paying passengers on anything large enough to carry them. Both owners and passengers, however, wanted to see engines resembling admired types in use on the main-line railways, and as they were not concerned with the carriage of goods, the odd-looking Heywood engines did not appeal to them.

The first locomotives with popular appeal appeared in amusement parks, fairgrounds and exhibitions in America, modelled on 4–4–0 No. 999 of the New York Central Railroad, which in 1893 had won international acclaim as the first locomotive to exceed 100 mph. A year later, four Irish-American brothers named Cagney formed their Miniature Railroad Company, and offered to supply steam locomotives of any type and for any gauge from 12⅝in. upwards, but principally to market models based on No. 999 in four gauges, 12⅝, 15, 18 and 22 inches. More than three thousand were built for them by two different manufacturers. One engine with a very special finish was supplied to the King of Siam. At least four came to Britain, the earliest appearing on exhibition tracks at Earls Court and in Glasgow in 1901.

The Cagney brothers had no need to exploit the full potential of the 15-inch gauge, and their locomotives, weighing less than one ton, were tiny in comparison with those built thirty years later. One of those that came to Britain was bought in 1903 by Charles Bartholomew, a civil engineer and railway enthusiast of Blakesley Hall, near Towcester, Northamptonshire, who laid a 15-inch gauge line from the Hall to Blakesley station on what later became known as the Stratford-on-Avon & Midland Junction Railway.

Like Heywood, he meant it to be enjoyed, but he intended it also to be useful in carrying visitors to the house and fuel to its electricity generating station. The Cagney engines, however, had been designed only for drawing light passenger trains, and Bartholomew soon found that his was not powerful enough to haul wagons laden with supplies up the 1 in 100 gradient leading from the railway station. In his own workshops in 1905 he therefore built an early example of an internal combustion locomotive, *Petrolea*, powerful but ugly.

Among his friends, however, was W.J. Bassett-Lowke who, after serving his apprenticeship with J.T. Lowke & Sons, engineers and boilermakers in Northampton, had set up his own firm to market model railway equipment far more realistic than any previously obtainable. The small sizes were manufactured for him by the renowned Nuremberg toymakers, Bing Brothers, but Bassett-Lowke intended to challenge the American monopoly of miniature passenger-carrying railways by building more powerful engines in his own Northampton factory. These were to be designed by a trained engineer, Henry Greenly, and after the two of them had studied Bartholomew's Cagney closely, Miniature Railways (Great Britain) Limited was formed in 1904 with help from local backers and the intention not only of building locomotives, but also of laying and operating lines in holiday resorts and exhibition grounds.

Greenly settled on a handsome Atlantic design with outside cylinders, for Atlantics were the express engines then used on the Lancashire & Yorkshire, Great Northern, North Eastern and Great Central railways. The first, suggestive of Wilson Worsdell's North Eastern engines with round-topped firebox and brass safety-valve cover, was completed in May 1905 and, after running trials on the well-laid track at Eaton Hall, *Little Giant* opened Miniature Railways' first venture, at South Shore, Blackpool, on Whit Monday, 10 June. There, on a level circuit a quarter of a mile long, her train of three or four open bogie carriages was well patronised by happy holiday-makers, nine thousand of whom were carried in a week.

On test at Eaton Hall, *Little Giant* had started a load of 12 tons without slipping, hauled the same weight at 5 mph on level track and with a light load on a descending gradient had reached a speed of 26 mph. Moreover, during the first week at Blackpool, she had covered more than a hundred miles, averaging some fifty-eight circuits a day without trouble. These were remarkable achievements for a prototype, proving soundness of design and excellence of workmanship.

More examples of what became known as Class 10 were built between 1908 and 1912: 14ft. 1½in. long, 2ft. 1in. wide, weight 1 ton 12 cwt., cost

Bassett-Lowke's Class 10 Atlantic, *Little Giant*, designed by Henry Greenly, is seen here on Miniature Railway's first pleasure ground line, opened at Blackpool South Shore on 10 June 1905. From a card postmarked Blackpool, 22 July 1905.

Little Giant was saved from destruction in 1966 and restored to working order. She is seen here in May 1988 on loan to the Ravenglass Railway Museum.

£345 with tender. Just how many there were is obscured by bewildering changes of site, name and livery, but a total of eight is thought probable: *Mighty Atom* was supplied to Sutton Park, Sutton Coldfield; *Entente Cordiale* to France for an exhibition at Nancy; *Red Dragon* and *Green Dragon* to The White City, Shepherd's Bush; three Kings, one of which was new, to an exhibition in Brussels; *George the Fifth* to the Southport Miniature Railway; *Hungaria* to Angol Park, Budapest.

Anxious to increase power so as to haul more passengers in each train at the amusement parks, Greenly designed the Improved Little Giant or Class 20 in 1911, with a larger boiler, superheated and working at a pressure increased from 120lb. to 125lb. per sq. in., and cylinders of greater diameter. Surprisingly, the advertised price was £320, less than that of the Class 10 engines. Only three are known to have been built: the first was sent in 1912 to the King of Siam, the second to the Southport Miniature Railway, and the third, built in 1914 and named *Prince Edward of Wales*, opened the Fairbourne Miniature Railway in 1916. Unlike the members of Class 10, which had an individual splasher over each driving wheel, those of Class 20 had one long splasher covering the pair.

However, in spite of so much ingenuity and activity, Miniature Railways had to go into liquidation in 1912, and its assets, four Class 10 engines, track, passenger carriages and other equipment, were advertised for sale. Nevertheless, Bassett-Lowke was able to acquire another partner, Robert Proctor Mitchell of the Polytechnic Tours Travel Agency, and form a new company, Narrow Gauge Railways, whose aim was to establish lines with a more substantial purpose – one might say 'real purpose' – carrying tourists and benefiting local inhabitants in a locality devoid of rail transport and, preferably, blessed with natural beauty.

Meantime, the most elegant of all miniature locomotives had been built for Charles Bartholomew with the beautifully balanced wheel arrangement of the 4–4–4 tank engine. *Blacolvesley* had appeared from the Northampton factory in 1909 fitted with a 12 h.p. petrol engine selected by Greenly so as not to impair the perfection of her outline. Leaving the Cagney to entertain visiting enthusiasts, *Blacolvesley* shared with *Petrolea* the humdrum task of hauling supplies from the standard gauge goods yard to the Hall, but as she could be made ready for use at a moment's notice, which the little steam engine could not, another of her duties was to fetch from the station visitors who had called up the Hall on Bartholomew's private telephone to ask for transport.

In 1911, Greenly developed his Atlantics still further, producing the *Sans Pareil* or Class 30, 2ft. longer, 4in. wider, with still larger cylinders (4⅛ ×

Blacolvesley on Charles Bartholomew's Blakesley Hall Railway. The 4–4–4 petrol-engined locomotive was designed by Henry Greenly and built by Bassett-Lowke at Northampton in 1909. From a Locomotive Publishing Company postcard.

6¾in.), and a longer boiler pressed to 130lb. per sq. in. Of course the weight was greater, 2 tons 5 cwt., and so was the price, £380. The appearance of Class 30 was distinctive, a one-quarter scale model based on the Atlantics designed by H.A. Ivatt for the Great Northern Railway with wide fireboxes. Again, only three examples were built. The first was bought by Sir Robert Walker of Sand Hutton, Yorkshire, in 1912 and named *Synolda* after his first wife. The second, *Sans Pareil*, was completed in 1913 for the exhibition railway in Luna Park, Geneva, but, as far as can be ascertained, it never went there and made its first appearance at the Oslo Exhibition in 1914, bearing the name *Prins Olaf*. Components for the third had been made before the Bassett-Lowke factory turned to making war material, and when these were assembled in 1924 with a boiler made by another Northampton firm, it was to the order of Count Louis Zborowski, a well-known racing driver, who was building a 15-inch gauge railway in Higham Park, his estate at Bridge near Canterbury; but little, if any, use did he make of it before he was killed racing in October 1924.

One more Bassett-Lowke 15-inch gauge engine remains to be mentioned, the only Pacific of the 'Colossus' or 'Gigantic' Class 60, built at Northampton in 1913 to the order of J.E.P Howey of Staughton Manor, Huntingdonshire, and named *John Anthony* after his baby son. Fitted with a far longer boiler working at 140lb. pressure, and weighing 3 tons, the engine cost £425. On test at Eaton Hall, she reached a speed of 35 mph, and started from rest a maximum load of 16 tons 14 cwt. made up of fifteen wagons and a brake van.

The miniature world of the 15-inch gauge was compact and tight knit. Most of its inhabitants were known to one another. Charles Bartholomew and W.J. Bassett-Lowke were friends; so also were Sir Robert Walker and Sir Arthur Heywood. Eskdale, Cumberland, was common ground to many of the men and locomotives already mentioned, for thither went *Ella* and *Muriel*, *Sans Pareil* and *Colossus*, W.J. Bassett-Lowke and Henry Greenly, Count Louis Zborowski and J.E.P. Howey. The Count's Atlantic went to Fairbourne; his shadow loomed behind Howey when establishing the most ambitious of all the 15-inch gauge railways at new Romney.

Several of the early engines have recovered their identity after strange vicissitudes that included the acquisition of fresh names on successive sites, of improbable disguises, even temporary oblivion. Oldest of the veterans still in working order is Sir Arthur Heywood's 0–8–0 *Muriel*, built in 1894; acquired by the Ravenglass & Eskdale Railway in 1917, a year after Sir Arthur's death, she was rebuilt in 1927 but still retained her Heywood chassis. Charles Bartholomew's Cagney has been found and restored, and so also has his *Blacolvesley*. The fate of *Synolda*, which had been sold when Sir Robert Walker developed a greater purpose, was unknown for many years, but eventually the disguise of an amusement park Atlantic was penetrated, and the dismembered remains identified as hers by the presence of a particular fitting; reconditioned at Ravenglass in 1980, she occasionally quits the Ravenglass Railway Museum for a gallop on the Eskdale tracks. The Class 10 built for Southport in 1911 and named *George the Fifth* was found beneath a heap of scrap metal, but is now in good hands. Most interesting of all, *Little Giant* herself was rescued in 1966 from a derelict amusement park the day before her remains were to be sold for scrap, but, restored to health, she was in steam at the Ravenglass & Eskdale Centenary Exhibition in September 1976, together with *Blacolvesley* and Count Louis Zborowski's Class 30 Atlantic.

CHAPTER TWO

THE 15-INCH GAUGE FAIRBOURNE RAILWAY

During my holiday at Llanuwchllyn, Merionethshire, with my father in August 1925, I visited several Welsh narrow gauge railways, as described elsewhere,★ and on the way back from the Talyllyn on 10 August there was, as I had hoped, time to break my journey from Towyn at Fairbourne in order to see the Fairbourne Miniature Railway – time to see, but alas! not time to ride.

Apart from its history and a spectacular backdrop of mountains beyond the Mawddach estuary, it had little claim to distinction. Nevertheless, it played a part, as did its contemporary, the Ravenglass & Eskdale, in the evolution of the Bassett-Lowke 15-inch gauge locomotive from a rich man's extravaganza running on a garden railway into a machine capable of working passenger-carrying trains to a public timetable. Furthermore, during the last twenty years of 15-inch gauge operation up to 1985, it played an influential part in the transformation of the very small engine from a model into a machine specially, and more suitably, designed for its purpose, becoming as much a narrow gauge locomotive in its own right as those of, for example, the Festiniog and Corris Railways.

The Afon Mawddach derives from a number of hill streams rising in the mountain area to the south-east of Ffestiniog and flows into the sea at Barmouth Bay, but the mouth of its estuary has been narrowed by a

★ Household, Humphrey, *Narrow Gauge Railways: Wales and The Western Front*, Gloucester: Alan Sutton, 1988.

peninsula of shingle and dunes reaching northward for two miles from Friog to Penrhyn Point, opposite the seaside resort of Barmouth. Narrow though the outlet is, above the bar the estuary is wide, and the main coast road from the south turns inland to cross the river at Penmaenpool or Dolgellau. To avoid this long detour of some 13 or 18 miles, of greater significance when transport depended on the horse, than it is today, a highway ran along the peninsula from Friog to a slip whence a ferry plied, as it still does for foot passengers, to Barmouth; so some form of transport from Friog to the ferry is of long standing.

Fairbourne itself, however, is of comparatively recent growth, a small offshoot from the development of Welsh seaside resorts that followed the building of the Cambrian Railways coast line and its bridge crossing the Mawddach estuary to Barmouth. In 1890 brickworks were established near the Cambrian line, and a 2ft. gauge tramway was laid from the works southward to the site of the future Fairbourne station, westward alongside the road leading to the beach, and northward along the seaward edge of the dunes and shingle towards Penrhyn Point. Along this tramway came horse-drawn wagons carrying to the building sites bricks from the kilns and other materials brought to a siding laid in by the Cambrian Railways. Once boarding houses and holiday homes had arisen on the way to the beach, and shops, a post office and a café near the railway, horse-drawn passenger cars began to run along Beach Road, and subsequently out to Penrhyn Point, for until the Cambrian opened Fairbourne station in 1912, Barmouth station and the ferry provided the best approach for holiday-makers arriving by rail.

Meanwhile, Narrow Gauge Railways Limited was looking for suitable sites on which to set up 15-inch gauge lines, and when the outbreak of war in August 1914 put an end to international exhibitions, it was essential to find those sites in Britain so that the company's stock of locomotives, carriages and rails would not lie idle. One had already been found in Eskdale in the summer of 1915, and a second was acquired by purchase of the Fairbourne tramway in 1916. As the portion from the brickworks to the Cambrian siding was no longer needed, it was abandoned, the remaining 1¾ miles were regauged, and the last of Bassett-Lowke's Class 20 engines was sent from Northampton with five four-wheeled open carriages.

The handsome little locomotive, presumably almost completed before the factory was commandeered for war work, had a polished brass dome and safety valve cover, and bore the name *Prince Edward of Wales* on her long splasher. Both she and the bogie tender accompanying her were painted green above the footplating and a reddish-brown below. Some of the four-wheeled carriages were fitted with glass screens as protection against

Fairbourne Miniature Railway: Bassett-Lowke Class 20 locomotive *Prince Edward of Wales* at the terminus among the sand dunes near Penrhyn Point, opposite Barmouth. From a Photochrom Co. Postcard. *c.* 1916.

smoke and cinders, and all could be rigged with canopies – which obviously would have been more effective in providing shade from hot sun than shelter from cold rain!

As *Prince Edward of Wales* was the only locomotive, traffic operation was simple, using the principle of 'one engine in steam'. Management was in the hands of John Wills, a solicitor with a love for model trains who was company secretary of Narrow Gauge Railways Limited and manager of the Bassett-Lowke emporium in High Holborn. Then in 1921, a group of ex-servicemen who had formed the Barmouth Motor Boat & Ferry Company leased the miniature railway to use it as one leg of a circular tour by ferry, road and rail. Unluckily, they were hit by two poor summers and, unable to meet their commitments, had to sell *Prince Edward of Wales* at the end of the 1923 season. She went to Llewellyn's Miniature Railway at Southport in exchange, presumably willy-nilly, for *Katie*, the only really wayward member of Sir Arthur Heywood's stud. Never a good steamer, yet hard worked for many years on the Eaton Hall Railway before going to Eskdale and then Southport, *Katie* plodded to and fro at Fairbourne, with

Bassett-Lowke Class 30 Atlantic, *Count Louis*, running on the Fairbourne Railway on 10 August 1925. The initials HR on the tender stand for Higham Railway, Count Louis Zborowski's garden railway at Higham Park, Bridge, near Canterbury, for which it was completed in 1924 shortly before the Count's death.

occasional halts to recover her breath, until one day her safety valve soared into the sky at Penrhyn Point, spectacularly ending her career. Except for frames and wheels, what remained was broken up in 1926.

In May 1924, Narrow Gauge Railways found itself in an embarrassing financial position, just as Miniature Railways (Great Britain) had done twelve years earlier. On this occasion rescue came from Sir Aubrey Brocklebank, chairman of T. & J. Brocklebank, shipowners, and a director of Cunard and the GWR amongst other companies. Living at Irton Hall, Cumberland, he had been interested in NGR's activity in Eskdale from an early stage and had provided much-needed capital. To protect his original investment, he and a partner now secured complete control, but preferring to limit their commitment to Sir Aubrey's neighbourhood, they sold the Fairbourne Miniature Railway to the Fairbourne Estate & Development Company from which the site had been leased.

John Wills remained as manager, and when it became obvious to the new owners that a reliable locomotive had to be found, his connection with Bassett-Lowke enabled him to obtain for them relatively cheaply one in first-class condition, for after the death of Count Louis Zborowski in October 1924, his Class 30 Atlantic was up for sale. She reached Fairbourne in time for Easter 1925 and, rightly named *Count Louis*, was still running with the initials of his Higham Railway roughly painted on her tender when I photographed her four months later.

The railway was then in a very simple, almost primitive, state. At the Fairbourne end, there was a shed for the locomotive and a loop for her to run around the carriages, but the train itself stood in the open beside Beach Road while passengers boarded or left. There were stopping places at Bathing Beach, where the route turned from west to north, Golf Links close to the Fairbourne Clubhouse, Penrhyn Point, and the terminus at Barmouth Ferry, where there was another running round loop amid the dunes and shingle. But as no turntables were provided, one trip had to be made tender first, the driver without shelter and having to look over his shoulder at the unfenced track ahead.

There were hazards. The author of an article which appeared in *The Locomotive* in 1942 remarked that after skirting the golf course, the trains crossed the line of play, so that Fairbourne 'is probably the only course in the country which has rules for the passage of a train across it', but he added that there was 'no record of a passenger being injured by an over zealous golfer'! Far more serious was the effect of the wind on such an exposed site, driving sand into the moving parts of the engine, damaging the bearings, and forming drifts across the track which made proper maintenance impossible. At the time of his visit before the outbreak of war in 1939, there were only three members of staff to keep an hourly service running, so it is not surprising that he found 'the standard of maintenance is not very high and consequently the running is rough'.★

An ill-judged attempt to ease the strain on *Count Louis* was made in 1926, when the Fairbourne Estate Company bought cheaply a model of Patrick Stirling's famous Great Northern Railway No. 1. It may be questioned whether such a high-stepping, single-driver locomotive was in any case suitable for hauling well-patronised miniature trains but, as her gauge was 18in., this model was in no way suitable! A certain amount of third rail was laid for her, but this was removed and the engine was sold in the mid-thirties. A better proposition was the purchase in 1935 of a 9 h.p. Lister petrol locomotive for use when *Count Louis* was out of action, as when she broke a connecting rod in 1939.

During the Second World War the Penrhyn and Fairbourne area, like other areas where dunes and shingle banks extended for some distance from the tide-line, was used for training troops in practice landings from the sea.

★ *The Locomotive Railway Carriage & Wagon Review*, Vol 48, 15 May 1942, pp. 96–7, article by R.A. Whitehead.

Exchanging single line tokens in the passing loop laid at Golf House in 1951. The driver of *Count Louis* holds in his left hand the staff he will give up and has extended his right arm to catch the loop of the next. From a postcard issued by the Fairbourne Railway Co.

By the end of the war, tracked amphibians, storm damage and neglect had reduced the miniature railway to such a deplorable state that restoration seemed unlikely. However, it had, after all, served a useful purpose in conjunction with the ferry. Moreover, there must have been many people who remembered the pleasure it had given them during childhood holidays. Perhaps the three business men from the Midlands who came to the rescue in 1946 had their memories; certainly they not only restored the Fairbourne Railway, but made it blossom as never before.

Piece by piece, the line was relaid towards the ferry, and as the steam locomotive was under repair, the Lister petrol engine hauled trains to the advancing railhead. *Count Louis* returned in time to work the summer service in 1947, and in 1948 restoration of the track reached the ferry terminus.

In that austere post-war era, holiday-makers had to be content with the amenities of British resorts, and the Fairbourne Railway was patronised by so many eager passengers that five new coaches, two of them enclosed, had to be added to the five Bassett-Lowke four-wheelers, and a second Lister locomotive obtained. Through the 1950s, the increasing traffic led to great improvements. The primitive Fairbourne terminus became a station indeed, with two platforms and four tracks under an overall roof. Colour light signals were installed, and a passing loop was provided near the golf clubhouse, with single line tokens controlling the movement of trains on either side of it. A four-coach articulated set, mounted on bogies, gave passengers a smoother ride, and three more internal combustion locomotives were obtained, two of them riding on bogies and all three fitted with Daimler engines.

But the most interesting development stemmed from the proprietors' faith in steam at a time when many miniature railways were totally abandoning it because internal combustion locomotives were more economical and could be brought into use more quickly. But knowing that steam engines had a far greater appeal to visitors young and old, and were quite capable of working the traffic efficiently, the proprietors of the Fairbourne Railway embarked on a series of experiments. First they borrowed a scale model of an LMS Stanier 'Black Five' 4–6–0, which had been designed by Ernest Twining and built at Stourbridge by the G & S Light Engineering Company for Dudley Zoo. Trial soon showed that to raise enough steam for regular service, it was essential to have a wider firebox, such as that fitted to another Dudley Zoo locomotive, a freelance Pacific built by the same firm in 1949. So the 'Black Five' was returned, and somewhat later the Pacific, named *Ernest W. Twining*, was borrowed instead. The next stage was to order a new engine specially suited to Fairbourne conditions and, abandoning the scale model concept, Twining designed a handsome and well-proportioned 2–4–2 with outside frames, a tall chimney, a large brass dome and a cab which gave the driver greater protection, very much a type of engine which could have been built by a British firm in the 1890s for service on a narrow gauge railway overseas – a 'Colonial' type. Delivered by the Stourbridge firm in 1963 and fitted with oil seals to exclude sand from her moving parts, *Sian* proved such a success that the Fairbourne partners took the opportunity to acquire her prototype. This was another *Katie*, a very different *Katie* to Heywood's, which had been built in 1957 for Dudley Zoo where steam had since been superseded.

The withdrawal of steam from railways in Britain, and indeed worldwide, has created widespread interest in the remaining examples of a machine so fascinatingly live and individual – for even locomotives of the same class show individuality in their behaviour. The result has been greater numbers visiting the surviving narrow gauge railways than were ever drawn to them, say, sixty years ago, and a corresponding development of those railways.

Dingo at Penrhyn: mounted on bogies and fitted with a 2½ litre Diamler petrol engine, it entered service at Fairbourne in 1951. From a postcard issued by the Fairbourne Railway Co.

No longer restricted to scale model proportions, the 2–4–2 *Sian* was designed by Ernest Twining and built for Fairbourne by Trevor Guest at Stourbridge in 1963, setting a precedent for future development of the 15-inch gauge steam locomotive. (*George Barlow.*)

During the second half of that period, the Fairbourne was indeed transformed, and it was unfortunate that the partners who had achieved so much found it necessary to withdraw. For several years the line faced a very uncertain future, until new proprietors were at last forthcoming. Sadly, the newcomers decided to abandon the 15-inch gauge and so much excellent equipment, and began to convert to 12¼in. after the close of the 1985 season. So *Sian* and *Katie* went elsewhere and received new names; but *Count Louis*, having earned honourable retirement after sixty years, was preserved at Fairbourne for a while before going to the Birmingham Railway Museum at Tyseley.

Was Sir Arthur Heywood mistaken, then, in his belief that the minimum gauge for the *satisfactory* conveyance of passengers and freight was 15 inches? Could a narrower gauge have sustained the mineral traffic in Eskdale, or the armoured train that patrolled the Romney Marshes? I doubt it.

CHAPTER THREE

THE RAVENGLASS & ESKDALE RAILWAY

Anyone who knows the Lake District and the dales opening westward to the Cumberland coast will realise how delighted Robert Proctor Mitchell and W.J. Bassett-Lowke would have been in finding in Eskdale an abandoned railway roadbed where they could use their 15-inch gauge material to benefit local inhabitants and open up to tourists a dale of great natural beauty.

The original Ravenglass & Eskdale Railway had been laid to a gauge of 3ft. and had been opened towards the end of May 1875 to serve haematite mines around Boot and Dalegarth, seven miles from Ravenglass. The dalesfolk of course soon asked for a passenger service, but besides building stations, a good deal had to be done to make a rough-and-ready mineral railway even passable for public use, and it was not until after Colonel Yolland, the Board of Trade inspecting officer, had examined it for the second time and imposed a speed limit of 10 mph, that the first passenger train could be run, on 20 November 1876.

However, mining of ironstone soon proved uneconomic, and as revenue from all sources was insufficient even to pay the contractor who had built the line, the affairs of the company were placed in the hands of a receiver little more than two years after the line had been opened. Nevertheless, the railway plodded on and, in spite of steady deterioration, carried granite setts from a quarry, local goods and passengers and appreciative tourists, until the end of November 1908, when it was closed for the first time. However, there were several attempts to revive mining and quarrying, leading to the

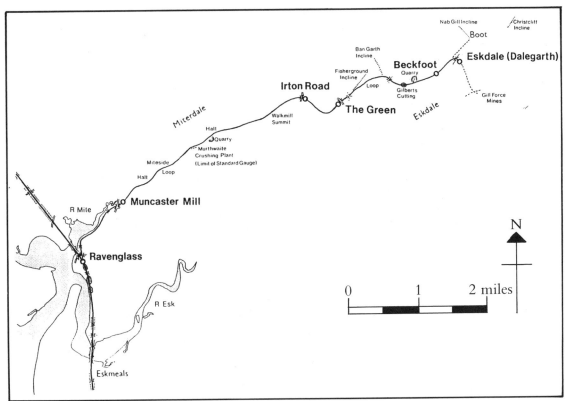

Map of the Ravenglass & Eskdale Railway. (*R & ER.*)

The 0–6–0 side tank locomotive *Devon*, built by Manning Wardle & Co., Leeds in 1875 for the 3ft. gauge railway at Boot about 1905. (*R & ER.*)

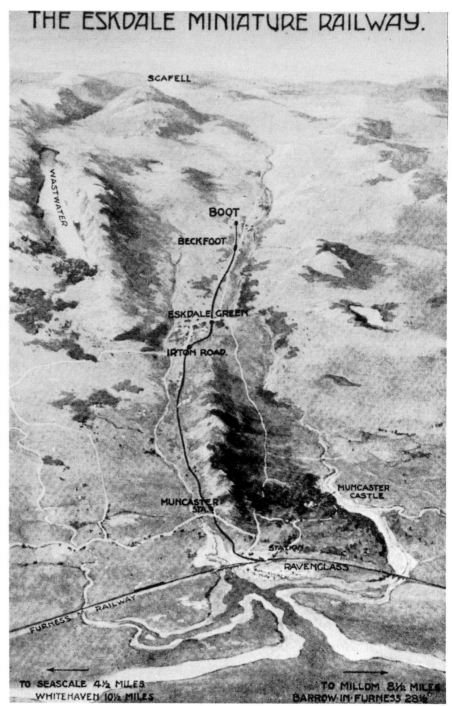

THE ESKDALE MINIATURE RAILWAY.

SCAFELL

WASTWATER

BOOT

BECKFOOT

ESKDALE GREEN

IRTON ROAD.

MUNCASTER CASTLE

MUNCASTER STA.

STATION

RAVENGLASS

FURNESS RAILWAY

TO SEASCALE 4½ MILES
WHITEHAVEN 10½ MILES

TO MILLOM 8½ MILES
BARROW-IN-FURNESS 28½

A 'hawk's-eye' representation of the railway and its environment. Of the three rivers flowing into the estuary at Ravenglass, Esk is on the right, Mite in the centre and Irt on the left. (*Locomotive Publishing Company*.)

Sans Pareil, built by Bassett-Lowke in 1913, at Muncaster Mill with covered bogie coach and brake van from Sir Arthur Heywood's Duffield Bank Railway, (*Locomotive Publishing Company.*)

railway being reopened for goods traffic only from May 1909 to mid-November 1910, and again in April 1911 until final closure on 30 April 1913.

Robert Proctor Mitchell may very well have heard of the abandoned line through his association with the Polytechnic Tours travel agency, which would certainly have covered the Lake District and Cumberland coast in the ordinary course of business. Visiting Eskdale early in 1915 and realising its possibilities in spite of steep gradients, sharp curves, overgrown track bed and derelict buildings, he returned in June with W.J. Bassett-Lowke and John Mills, the secretary of the Narrow Gauge Railways Company. Liking what they saw, they acted quickly, leasing the site a month later. Its only serious disadvantage was that the Cumberland coast and its dales were then comparatively unknown and, lying well to the west of the London & North Western Railway main line from Lancaster to Carlisle, could be reached only by changing to the Furness Railway at Carnforth, whence the trains followed a circuitous course round coast, estuaries and the Barrow peninsula before reaching Ravenglass.

Ravenglass itself stands on a curiously shaped estuary into which flow the rivers Esk, Mite and Irt, and it was, and is, Miterdale which the railway first followed, climbing for just over four miles to cross the northern end of

Muncaster Fell near Irton Road before entering Eskdale. But whoever chose the original route had not maintained a steady descent for the laden mineral trains, which were faced with half a mile at 1 in 63/64 from Eskdale Green to Irton Road and a sharp 1 in 40 approaching Ravenglass. Returning trains of empty wagons of course climbed most of the way, but at five points the gradient was between 1 in 42 and 1 in 48, and at another there was a short stretch of 1 in 36. Evidently, however, Mitchell and Bassett-Lowke were confident that these gradients were not beyond the capacity of a one-quarter scale model Atlantic hauling a light passenger train.

The locomotive was the second of Class 30, which had been sent to the Oslo Exhibition in 1914 bearing the name *Prins Olaf* but, after the outbreak of war in August, had been marooned in Norway together with seven open four-wheeled carriages. Now that a place to use them had been found, instructions were sent for despatch direct to Ravenglass, where the work of clearing the overgrown way and re-gauging the track had already begun, using the original rails and the sound centre part of the old sleepers.

Surprisingly, considering what was going on across the Channel and on the high seas, all went according to plan. The Oslo equipment arrived sometime during August, the engine was renamed *Sans Pareil*, and on 28 August trains began to run along a mile of line from Ravenglass to Muncaster Mill – little more than a month after the signing of the lease! Extension to Irton Road followed on 1 February 1916, to Eskdale Green on 1 April, to Beckfoot on 8 June, and finally to Boot in April 1917. This created a need for more locomotives and rolling stock, almost impossible to obtain in wartime. Sir Arthur Heywood was approached, but refused to part with *Ella* or *Muriel*, although he did sell three enclosed bogie vehicles, invaluable if services were to be run during the winter.

However, the one and only Pacific of Bassett-Lowke's Class 60 had, like *Prins Olaf*, become marooned. In July 1914, J.E.P. Howey had taken *John Anthony* to the Duke of Westminster's Eaton Hall Railway for tests that were impracticable on his own Staughton Manor line. Leaving her there while he went shooting in Scotland, he never returned to collect her, for he was mobilised with the Bedfordshire Yeomanry. He soon transferred to the Royal Flying Corps and, crash landing in enemy territory, became a prisoner of war. So *John Anthony* had remained in the Duke of Westminster's engine shed, well cared for but unused.

There the impressive little locomotive, so obviously suitable as a companion for *Sans Pareil*, was seen by Proctor Mitchell when he went to Eaton Hall to make an offer for *Katie* which, he had been told, was about to be replaced by a new Heywood engine. Correspondence with Howey found

Colossus, built by Bassett-Lowke in 1913 for J.E.P. Howey, receiving attention in preparation for the day's work, watched by an admiring schoolboy wearing one of those curious felt hats which were *de rigueur* for school cricket in those days! At Ravenglass, 11 August 1924.

him ready to sell, so before the opening of the summer season in 1916 the Ravenglass & Eskdale acquired both *Katie* and *John Anthony*. Then came the death of Sir Arthur and the auction of all his railway material at the end of May. This was bought by a dealer, who re-sold four open bogie carriages, the sleeping car and some of the wagons to Ravenglass, but in whatever he intended to do with the rest of the equipment, he was frustrated by the Ministry of Munitions which commandeered track and locomotives for use while building an ordnance factory at Gretna Green.

Of course, the formation of a 15-inch gauge railway for a serious purpose in Eskdale attracted a good deal of publicity, especially in the pages of *The Railway Magazine* and *The Locomotive Railway Carriage & Wagon Review*, and the Locomotive Publishing Company issued six coloured postcards, black-and-white photographs painted by 'F. Moore', a set of which I obtained in February 1916. It is of considerable interest historically: one card is a pictorial

Heywood's 0–6–0 *Ella* at Ravenglass in 1924. (*R & ER.*)

Ella with a freight train loaded with sacks of wool. The rails are obviously those of the old mineral railway re-gauged on the original sleepers. (*R & ER.*)

map of the line and the district; four depict *Sans Pareil* at work, in one case hauling Heywood's covered bogie coach and brake van; and the sixth shows the Class 60 Pacific, not indeed in Eskdale, but posed outside Staughton Manor with Howey as driver. However, the photograph from which 'F. Moore' worked had been retouched; the original lettering on tender and splasher had been erased, and *John Anthony* had become *Gigantic*, the name chosen by Bassett-Lowke for inclusion in his catalogue entry. Others thought differently, however, but as the need for her services was urgent, she ran for a time in Eskdale clearly marked as *John Anthony* of the Staughton Manor Railway, before herself acquiring the name *Colossus* and her tender the initials NGR.

The arrival of two more engines relieved the pressure on *Sans Pareil* but did not solve the problem of how to move the increasing number of holiday-makers visiting Eskdale for rides on this intriguing little railway. When demand was heaviest, the wayward *Katie* was used to haul four-wheeled wagons furnished with benches but, the climb up the dale exhausting her, she would come to a halt, and passengers would gather wild flowers, berries or mushrooms while she recovered! Even when her two respectable sisters, *Ella* and *Muriel*, became available, there was still a need for more power, as the railway was carrying not only passengers, but also freight: timber and wool outward, coal and groceries inward for the valley residents.

Clearly a new locomotive was essential but, in spite of the tourists, net receipts were insufficient to cover the cost, and there was therefore no possibility of obtaining one unless paid for by someone outside the company. Sir Aubrey Brocklebank, the wealthy shipowner living nearby at Irton Hall, had already provided some capital, secured by an issue of debentures, and he now agreed to increase his investment. As Bassett-Lowke no longer manufactured 15-inch gauge locomotives, the order for another Pacific was placed with Hunt & Co., a Bournemouth firm engaged in light engineering which had never built a locomotive before, nor ever did again.

The engine was intended to be based on Greenly's *Colossus*, but at that date the railway had an enigmatic consulting engineer named Cauchi, and Greenly objected to another man using his working drawings – as he did later at New Romney. Appeal to the High Court for an injunction was only just averted, and Greenly was persuaded to allow the *Sans Pareil* drawings to be used instead. Up to a point these were, but the decision to build to a quarter of the continental, rather than the British, loading gauge, allowed a larger boiler to be mounted, with the higher working pressure of 150lb. per

Sans Pareil alongside Ravenglass station, 11 August 1924. Robert Proctor Mitchell speaking to the driver.

Sir Aubrey Brocklebank, built by Hunt & Co., Bournemouth, 1919, on the turntable at Ravenglass on 11 August 1924.

sq. in. The measurements of wheels and cylinders, however, were the same as those of *Sans Pareil* and *Colossus*, and the weight was only about 5 cwt. greater.★ The boiler was made by an experienced firm of boilermakers, and Hunt & Co. built with craftsmen's skill and pride, so the engine, completed in 1919 and named *Sir Aubrey Brocklebank*, gave good service, her only fault lying in the design of the firebox, supposedly due to Cauchi.

Sir Aubrey looked further than the provision of another engine. As granite had been drawn from a quarry at Beckfoot during the first decade of the twentieth century, perhaps granite could provide the mineral traffic the railway so badly needed to improve its earnings. In 1922, therefore, he formed the Beckfoot Quarry Company to produce roadstone and paving setts, and commissioned Henry Greenly to design a crushing plant. This was built in 1922–3 on a site where it would be as unobtrusive as possible, at Murthwaite, tucked into the wooded flank of Muncaster Fell, 2½ miles from Ravenglass and 4½ from the quarry.

Hauling laden mineral trains against adverse gradients was not suitable work for scale model locomotives which, after all, had been bred from stock designed for garden railways and amusement parks with easy gradients or none. As it was, *Sans Pareil* and *Colossus* had found the 1 in 38 beyond Beckfoot too much for them, and the final stretch of the railway to the old terminus at Boot, converted to the 15-inch gauge in April 1917, had to be abandoned less than eighteen months later and a less demanding terminus chosen, first at Beckfoot and then in 1922 just over a quarter of a mile beyond, at Dalegarth Cottages on the branch to the old Gill Force mine.

The design of the Heywood engines was better suited to heavy haulage, but only over short distances with halts between trips during which the launch-type boiler could regenerate steam, not runs of several miles as in Eskdale. Moreover, of the three acquired by the R & ER, *Katie* had been sold in 1918; *Muriel*, although thoroughly overhauled in 1921–2 and improved by reduction of cylinder volume, remained handicapped by her ageing and inadequate boiler; and both she and *Ella* were being so hard-worked handling the granite that extensive reconstruction was bound to be necessary before long.

Greenly was therefore asked to design a locomotive especially for the mineral traffic. Working with Proctor Mitchell, now designated General

★ Published figures of working pressure and weight are not consistent, some of the confusion arising from the fact that the boiler pressure of the new engine was raised experimentally from 150lb. to 180lb. in 1922; but as that was not a success, it reverted to 150lb. a year later.

Manager and himself an experienced engineer, Greenly produced drawings for a powerful 2–8–2 weighing 6 tons 18 cwt., with 17½in. driving wheels, cylinders 5¼in. diameter with 8½in. stroke, a boiler with a heating surface of 19,348 sq. in. (that of the new Pacific was 12,034 sq. in.) and a pressure of 180lb. per sq. in. – the same pressure as used on many British main-line engines, including Nigel Gresley's Pacific *Great Northern*. To achieve this, Greenly broke away from the one-quarter size he had previously adhered to and adopted one-third full size. Indeed, he had wanted to go further and produce a 'super Heywood', though with a conventional locomotive boiler and a cab that would shelter the driver, but Mitchell still clung to the concept of model proportions. Between the two of them and the builders, Davey Paxman & Co. of Colchester, a handsome and powerful engine was completed in 1923, though with one blemish, for at the suggestion of the builders, *River Esk* was fitted with Lentz poppet valves and Paxman Patent Valve Gear, which did not prove satisfactory. Mitchell was probably wise in insisting on a 'model' outline: in 1923 there were still plenty of narrow gauge railways with steam locomotives of such strange appearance that appreciation was an acquired taste, whereas the appeal of the Eskdale scale models was immediate – and, after all, it was not only the splendour of the scenery that led crowds to brave Lake District rain in open carriages!

★   ★   ★

In August 1924, we spent a family holiday at Brimmer Head Farm in Easedale, north-west of Grasmere, and I delightedly planned a visit to Eskdale, though how to get there was a problem unresolved for some days. We had brought a bicycle, and with its help, two routes appeared possible: one, direct from Ambleside to Beckfoot by a road of doubtful quality and intimidating names, Wrynose Bottom and Hard Knott Pass; the other, over Red Bank to Coniston and thence by what was still in essentials the Furness Railway, changing from branch to main line at Foxfield. Having to face a gruelling twenty-mile ride-cum-walk over Hard Knott and Wrynose passes at the end of a long day seemed unwise, so I chose instead the thirteen-mile ride to Coniston where the bicycle could be left at the station. This had the advantage that I would first see the miniature railway at its base, Ravenglass, and afterwards as far up the dale as time would permit for, as with all these narrow gauge railways, I went not merely for the ride, but to see what traffic was carried and how it was handled – in this case, the granite at Murthwaite.

The previous May, the legality of the lease by which Narrow Gauge Railways had acquired use of the mining railway's property had been

River Esk as built by Davey Paxman & Co., Colchester in 1923 with Lentz poppet valves and Paxman Patent Valve Gear. Alongside the transhipment viaduct at Ravenglass on 11 August 1924.

questioned, and to protect his now considerable investment, Sir Aubrey Brocklebank had settled the subsequent claims, and then, with a partner, Henry Lithgow, a Clydeside shipbuilder, had secured entire control. He was later to install new officers who introduced great changes, but that was not until early 1925, and so the Ravenglass & Eskdale Railway I saw was still the large scale model railway set up by W.J. Bassett-Lowke, Robert Proctor Mitchell and Henry Greenly – the 'amateur professionals' W.J.K. Davies not unfairly dubbed them. Happy-go-lucky and haphazard in its operation, it was by no means free from accident, but it was picturesque, unsophisticated and endearing.

Shunting, or strengthening a train with extra vehicles, was often done by hand. Vacuum brakes were fitted, but how extensively these were used is another question. There were signals at one or two stations, but there was no systematic signalling and, when traffic was heavy, Proctor Mitchell and his Superintendent of the Line, Robert Hardie (who later went to New

Sans Pareil and *Sir Aubrey Brocklebank* arriving at Ravenglass from Dalegarth on 11 August 1924.

River Esk leaving Ravenglass with the 12.30 p.m. to Dalegarth, 11 August 1924, with steam leaking from the valves. In the background, on the left, wisps of steam rise from *Colossus* outside the engine shed.

Romney), acted as pilotmen so that Up and Down trains could pass in loops at Murthwaite or Irton Road. Each locomotive carried a white disc in front of the chimney, as did those in the south-east to denote route and classification. Of course, neither route nor classification had any significance in Eskdale, but the disc had its uses, as white could be changed for red to indicate that the train was running in more than one portion, and this warning was repeated on the tail of the last vehicle. Youth was much in evidence among the operating staff: a lad cleaning *Colossus* was no doubt being trained as a driver. Schoolboys on holiday were certainly acting as guards.

There was a winter service, sustained by a Royal Mail contract and operated by peculiar internal combustion machines, which were useful also for permanent way maintenance. One was a wooden four-wheeled chassis fitted with a 4 h.p. Douglas motor-cycle engine; another had a 2 h.p. twin-cylinder two-stroke petrol engine; a third, which I saw and made a note of, 'appeared to be a modified Ford car mounted to run on rails'. This was, in fact, a 'Crewe Tractor', more than 130 of which had been built for the War Department in the LNWR Crewe Works following a suggestion made by one of the staff – or as some say, by a daughter of the Chief Mechanical Engineer, C.J. Bowen Cooke! Basically, it was a Ford Model T car mounted on a four-wheeled 60cm. gauge underframe, which could be raised or lowered so that the vehicle could run either on such roads as still survived behind the Western Front or on the very light rail tracks reaching forward positions. A turning-plate was incorporated which could be lowered to lift the contraption off the rails and enable it to be swung round ready for the return journey. The Eskdale example was, of course, permanently fixed to its rail mounting but it retained the turning plate although that was unpopular because on the narrower gauge the tractor was unstable while being swung. Exuberant driving of all the R & E petrol-engined machines (there were others later) resulted in not infrequent collisions.

I reached Ravenglass well before the 11.20 a.m. train left for Dalegarth, double-headed. To my delight, all four scale models were in use that day, and during the next three hours I was able to photograph them at Ravenglass: *Sans Pareil* at the station, Robert Proctor Mitchell standing beside her while speaking to the driver; *Colossus* outside the engine shed, being prepared for the day's work; *River Esk* ready to back down to the 12.30 p.m. train; *Sir Aubrey Brocklebank* on the turntable after arriving from Dalegarth at 1.05. *Sans Pareil* and *Colossus* had lost the Royal Blue livery shown on the early postcards and, like *Sir Aubrey*, had been painted red; although some say it was Midland Red, my recollection is of the attractive

The Murthwaite Crushing Plant, showing the sector table giving access to the seven sidings for the seven grades of stone. 11 August 1924.

The wagon tippler on the viaduct at Ravenglass from which stone was discharged into LMS wagons below. 11 August 1924.

Indian Red used by the Furness Railway from which, as relations were friendly, the paint might have been obtained. *River Esk* was a greyish green.

Making for Murthwaite, I left on the 1.50, drawn by *Colossus*. It is a long time ago, but I feel certain that the train made a special stop to set me down at Murthwaite, probably arranged by the traffic superintendent, Bob Hardie, as a kindly gesture to a keenly interested teenager. I was just in time to photograph *Ella* as she propelled ten laden wagons up the incline towards the stone embankment and concrete viaduct carrying the high-level sidings from which the crushing plant was fed. I did not see inside the building, but outside there were the revolving screens delivering seven grades of crushed stone into hoppers above a fan of sidings. To avoid elaborate pointwork for which there was not enough space, each of the seven sidings led to a sector table, like half a turntable pivoted at one end, by which one wagon at a time was transferred to or from the trunk siding – a neat but time-consuming operation. Yes, Murthwaite was certainly what W.J.K. Davies called it, 'a beautiful model-engineering-style crushing plant',* but it was no 'model' stone that it crushed, and the adamant granite took its toll.

Down at Ravenglass, transhipment of stone from the narrow gauge was by a 'tippler' on a viaduct above an LMS siding. The tippler and the steel doorless wagons, or 'stone hutches', had been made by Francis Theakston Ltd., a firm which specialised in equipment for light railways and had provided much material for the 60cm. gauge railways used on the Western Front. It consisted of three rings joined longitudinally by pairs of angle irons, the lower pair forming the 15-inch track for the 'hutch', the upper pair clasping it by the top as it was rolled sideways, discharging its contents into the standard gauge wagon below. Bottom-door wagons could also discharge direct, two at a time, side by side, through spaces between the rails, into one main-line wagon beneath. The crushed granite was sent away for use as roadstone, or by the LMS as track ballast.

I had spent so much time at Murthwaite that I could do no more than walk to Eskdale Green station to catch the last train back to Ravenglass. On a low grass-grown platform there stood a ramshackle timber waiting room where tattered strips of paper flapped from North Eastern Railway poster boards, a survival from the days of the original 3ft. gauge railway, as were all the stations except the new upper terminus. Presently the 5 p.m. from Dalegarth arrived behind *River Esk*, which during the summer season was often to be seen heading passenger trains. My photographs of her drawing into Eskdale

---

* Davies, W.J.K., *The Ravenglass & Eskdale Railway*, p. 65.

River Esk arriving at the dilapidated station at Eskdale Green, 11 August 1924.

Even a 15-inch gauge train could slip coaches! In the summers of 1922–3 the 11.15 a.m. ran non-stop to Dalegarth and slipped coaches at Irton Road for passengers intending to join motor coach tours. (*R & ER: Mary Fair.*)

Green station and leaving Ravenglass show a splendid machine, but show also an alarming loss of steam through the poppet valves.

So much for August 1924. Early in 1925, Sir Aubrey Brocklebank's measures to improve operation and increase earnings began to take shape. In February Mitchell resigned, and as W.J. Bassett-Lowke, although maintaining a keen interest, was fully engaged in managing his Northampton business, the two pioneers had little further influence. Sir Aubrey moved the company's registered office from Ravenglass to the Cunard Building in Liverpool, and his new General Manager, William Gillon, was a Liverpool man. As engineer, he appointed Ted Wright, with Tom Jones as assistant.

Perhaps the eye of an eighteen-year-old was too uncritical to notice signs of the wasteful and inefficient management that prevailed before Gillon took charge, but in the words of W.J.K. Davies, what the newcomers found 'amounted to a state of chaos'.* There was, for example, such a shortage of rolling stock that during the summer season even the stone hutches had to be pressed into service, but though these could be furnished with seats of a kind, they had no doors, so entry must have been very awkward, especially for anyone wearing a skirt! Yet the Heywood sleeping car and bogie brake van, which could easily have been adapted for regular use, lay neglected.

The track had never been given enough attention. The formation was that made in the 1870s for a railway intended to carry minerals only, so earthworks had been as light as possible with switchback gradients and severe curves. Yet when the line was re-gauged in 1915–17, little was done to ease slope or curve. Old rails had been used as they were, many well worn, especially at the ends. From 1922 onwards through the twenties there was gradual improvement: new flat-bottomed rails weighing 25lb. or 30lb. per yard were laid on timber sleepers set more closely and better ballasted. After 1925, cutting and filling reduced some of the abrupt changes of gradient, and new alignment eased some of the worst curves.

The Murthwaite plant had to be rebuilt, for when the Royal Mail contract was lost in 1927, there was only one way of avoiding total closure during the winter months, and that was by boosting the mineral traffic and handling it more economically. To achieve this, a new crushing plant of stronger construction, driven by a more powerful oil engine, was installed, and the screens were reset at right angles so as to feed wagons on one long siding instead of seven short ones. The sector table was removed, and the hutches were replaced by bogie hopper wagons with bottom doors for direct discharge from the viaduct at Ravenglass. The work was carried out in

* Davies, W.J.K., *The Ravenglass & Eskdale Railway*, p. 68.

Ella with a Bank Holiday Special in the original Ravenglass station about 1923: such a shortage of coaching stock that some of Theakston's doorless 'stone hutches' had to be used. (*R & ER.*)

Reverse curvature between mountainside and river in upper Eskdale, beyond Fisherground looking towards Beckfoot. A neat piece of well-laid modern track. 14 May 1987.

6-ton all-steel bogie wagons in Ravenglass goods yard. Built by the Yorkshire Engine Co. in 1928, these were later bought by the Romney Hythe & Dymchurch Railway, and two were used in the armoured train on that line. (*R & ER: Mary Fair.*)

1927–8, six all-steel bogie wagons, each with a capacity of 6 tons, being delivered from the Yorkshire Engine Co. in May 1928. Yet, in all this the new management showed an extraordinary lack of foresight, because scarcely were the new methods in operation before another plan was adopted: for, by laying a standard gauge track to Murthwaite, transhipment of graded stone at Ravenglass could be avoided altogether.

These further alterations were carried out remarkably rapidly, between 4 March and 21 November 1929, although they involved widening the formation, lifting the rails, replacing the short sleepers by longer ones, re-laying narrow gauge rails between those of standard gauge, and erecting a new bridge to give the standard gauge track entry to Ravenglass. Nevertheless, the 15-inch gauge rails were in position ready for the tourist trains at Whitsun, the start of the season. For the interlacing of the gauges beyond the Ravenglass yard and their separation approaching Murthwaite, unusual pointwork had to be designed, because the gaps essential for the flanges of standard gauge wheels would be far too wide for 15-inch stock to cross with safety. The 'Big Points', as they became known, therefore consisted of two short pieces of rail, pivoted so that they could be moved to give continuous support to the wheels of a train of either gauge, and set by a trackside lever

Northern Rock approaching Dalegarth station with the directors' special on 11 May 1988. When the terminus was moved in 1926 from Dalegarth Cottages, originally built for the ore miners and seen in the background, to the present terminus beside the valley road, the tracks followed the route of the old Gill Force mine branch between its fine dry stone walls.

interlocked with a signal. To haul the standard gauge wagons, a six-coupled locomotive with a 90 h.p. diesel engine was obtained from Kerr Stuart & Co. of Stoke-on-Trent.

At Ravenglass, the station was badly in need of reconstruction, as the old timber train shed was by then very dilapidated. It had covered one 3ft. gauge line alongside the platform, but although it had been possible to lay two of the narrower tracks beneath, these were not enough on busy days, so a third train had to stand in the open, and passengers seeking seats strolled dangerously to and fro across the rails. During the winter of 1927–8, the site was therefore cleared, and four tracks, neatly ballasted, were laid, all converging on the turntable. Three lines served new platform faces, and the fourth was for the release of locomotives after they had been turned.

At the other end of the line, the terminus, which had already been shifted from Boot to Beckfoot and Beckfoot to Dalegarth Cottages, was shifted again in 1926 to a point beyond the Whillan Beck, conveniently close to the valley road. Three tracks led to the turntable, one beside the platform,

Irton Road station and bridge, repaired, but little altered, between 1875 and 1987.

Miteside Halt, half a mile beyond Muncaster, where a footpath crosses the track and drops down to a footbridge over the river, seen between the trees on the extreme left. The original shelter formed by the bows of an ancient boat became such a well-known lineside feature that, when it decayed beyond repair, a similar boat section had to be found to replace it. Trains will call if you give an arm signal! 14 May 1988.

another as standage for carriages, and the third for engines to run round. A pavilion was installed on the platform to house an office and a café, supported on piles because of the sloping ground. Even so, the position was so cramped that the centre track was removed six years later.

Elsewhere, platform shelters gently rotted away, as at Eskdale Green – all, that is, except Irton Road's, sturdily built of stone and still in 1988 much as it was in the 1870s.

By the late twenties, much of the coaching stock needed replacing. Bassett-Lowke's open four-wheelers had been solidly constructed and nicely finished with oak underframes, and teak bodies varnished and lined in blue and gold (price in 1914, £52 10s. each, vacuum brake included). However, all had been built in 1912 – seven for the exhibition railway, four for Sir Robert Walker's Sand Hutton Railway – and all had suffered from exposure to the weather as there was no carriage shed before the early 1920s. Sir Arthur Heywood's bogie coaches had also suffered, and although several of his covered ones had been rebuilt and three similar vehicles added, more new stock was badly needed. Six open bogie carriages were built at Ravenglass in 1928, and another twelve in 1932–5.

The locomotive department was in no happier state. The engines built for the 3ft. gauge had been far better able to endure the rough state of the track than the early scale models. Moreover, the latter had been overworked in service never contemplated when they had been built, with the result that frames had cracked, boilers were strained, and failures had become altogether too frequent. *River Esk*, although handicapped by her inefficient valve gear, had therefore to handle an increasing number of passenger trains, while *Ella* and *Muriel*, neither in the best of condition, worked the stone trains from Beckfoot to Murthwaite and Murthwaite to Ravenglass. *Sans Pareil*, worn out, was withdrawn at the end of the 1926 season; *Colossus* could not last much longer.

Ted Wright's difficulty must have been where to begin rather than what to do, for he had ideas: articulation of steam engines was one, use of internal combustion locomotives was another. He began with *River Esk*, sending her away early in 1927 to the Yorkshire Engine Co. to have her poppet valves replaced by conventional Walschaerts valve gear, and, at the firm's suggestion, her tender converted into a two-cylinder power unit on the Poultney patent system. She returned in mid-January 1928 with a tender perched above eight coupled wheels, and after trials and adjustments, re-entered service a month later.

Next, it was *Muriel*'s turn. Her Heywood chassis was perfectly sound, so a new boiler was obtained from the same firm (working pressure 165lb. per sq. in.) and her frame lengthened to take a pair of trailing wheels under a wide firebox. But a bold attempt to make her resemble a scale model was unfortunate: the cab with its side windows looked nice, but it was so low that the driver had rather less protection than that given by the Heywood weather shield, while a short chimney instead of the original tall one, increased his discomfort. Besides, there was no way of disguising the width of the running plate, so that from the front the locomotive appeared clumsily proportioned. However, even though Ted Wright had shown little aesthetic appreciation, he had produced an excellent locomotive. She reappeared in traffic at the beginning of August 1927 as *River Irt*, and is still active now.

The two Pacifics, *Colossus* and *Sir Aubrey Brocklebank*, were withdrawn in November 1927, with the intention of using their chassis in the construction of another articulated locomotive. For this, the Yorkshire Engine Co. supplied a new boiler with a wide and deep Belpaire firebox and a working pressure of 180lb. per sq. in. This was joined by massive rigid side frames to a tender and cab fashioned at Ravenglass, and the whole was pivoted on bearing plates fitted to the two chassis shorn of their trailing axles. But the 4–6–0 + 0–6–4 articulated *River Mite* was of distressing ugliness. There was no way of concealing those prominent side frames, though the impact would have been less had the twenty-five rivet heads been either smaller or countersunk. Nevertheless, the boiler successfully fed four cylinders, providing the railway in May 1928 with a powerful engine capable of hauling heavy passenger or mineral trains.

Ella experienced a metamorphosis, for although she retained her Heywood 0–6–0 chassis, she emerged as a 2–6–2 driven by a petrol engine! Lengthened by 2ft. at each end to take the extra axle, she was fitted with part of a Lanchester touring car, complete with six-cylinder engine and gearbox coupled to a Parson's Marine Reverse, so that she could run equally well in either direction. With a wooden body and central cab, and known as ICL No. 2, she was set to work in the spring of 1927 and proved very useful.

The Crewe Tractor had been virtually destroyed in the autumn of 1925 when the magneto fractured and the flywheel broke loose, but parts were used in creating ICL No. 1. The old four-wheeled frame was lengthened, the extension carried on a two-axle bogie, and another Ford Model T engine fitted. A respectable teak body was superimposed, having, like *Ella*, a central cab. Unfortunately, the two ICLs collided in October 1928, smashing No. 1's body and straining No. 2's frame. Provision of another home-made body proved easier than straightening a distorted frame, but what remained of *Ella* continued in use until the spring of 1929, when a fractured big-end and split crankcase ended her career – but not that of the indestructible

Heywood's *Muriel* was rebuilt with a new boiler in 1927 and renamed *River Irt*, but the attempt to make her resemble the scale models by reducing the size of cab, dome and chimney was misguided. At Irton Road. (*R & ER: Mary Fair.*)

River Mite, the articulated engine constructed at Ravenglass in 1927–8 out of the chassis of *Colossus* and *Sir Aubrey Brocklebank* and a new boiler from the Yorkshire Engine Co. But oh, those rivets! (*R & ER: Mary Fair.*)

Heywood chassis! One other peculiar machine existed in 1927–30: a Scooter, known as *The Scot* from its twin-cylinder two-stroke Scott Squirrel engine; this was much used for maintaining communication between Ravenglass, the Murthwaite Crushing Plant and Beckfoot Quarry. It was surprisingly popular with the staff, who appreciated its ability to 'scoot' up to 50 mph, although it had no brakes (no wonder the ICLs were accident-prone!).

By the late 1920s, effective internal combustion tractors were available commercially. Three were ordered from Muir-Hill Service Equipment Ltd., Trafford Park Works, Manchester, who were supplying four-wheeled tractors for railways of various gauges, fitting them with Fordson 20 h.p. engines which started up on petrol before changing to the much cheaper paraffin.* Gearbox and chain drive provided two speeds in each direction. The first was delivered in January 1928 and the others in April 1929. After standard gauge rails reached Murthwaite, their work was limited to stone trains between Beckfoot and the crushing plant, and two of them were engaged in this for more than twenty years (one is now preserved in Ravenglass Museum). The third was reconstructed about 1933 with length-ened frames and a bogie for working passenger trains – and dolled up with cab, chimney, and what purported to be bunker and side tanks, to look like nothing that was ever moved by steam!

When I wrote 'Some notes on the Eskdale Railway' based on what I had seen in August 1924, I was unaware of these later developments. I had written to Ravenglass at the end of April 1926, asking for recent informa-tion, but received no reply. The 'notes' appeared as a short article in *The Locomotive Railway Carriage & Wagon Review* for April 1927, that is before the Murthwaite plant had been rebuilt, *River Esk* had acquired her steam tender, the Pacifics had become the articulated *River Mite* or the Heywoods had been reconstructed. Yet the management wrote an angry letter to the Editor, saying in no uncertain terms that my article did not portray the railway as it then was. But, as the Editor said in a soothing letter to me, my article had never claimed to do more than record my 1924 impressions. Obviously the management was over-sensitive to any mention of the earlier operating methods, but I still wonder what it was that caused such offence: cinders in the eyes of passengers? drivers looking like sweeps at the end of a trip? Perhaps 'schoolboys on holiday acting as guards' caused most annoyance; yet I had written enthusiastically about the handling of the granite traffic.

---

* From information supplied by the Muir-Hill company in 1927–8 concerning a tractor supplied to the Weston Clevedon & Portishead Railway.

Certainly, in the few years following 1925, the management had created a railway better organised and equipped, but this would not have been possible without the enthusiastic support – and the cash – of Sir Aubrey Brocklebank. When he died on 19 April 1929, it was as though the heart of the enterprise had also ceased to beat, for neither his son nor his partner had the same interest or the same readiness to invest. What works had been begun were carried to completion, but not even expansion of the quarrying appeared likely to be really profitable, and so its output remained limited to what the LMS was prepared to take for ballasting.

In the words of W.J.K. Davies, through the thirties 'the line went into a slow but steady decline'.* Ted Wright's daring experiments with articulation had not proved successful. *River Esk* discarded her hump-backed tender in 1931, thereby regaining her original dignified appearance. Patent notwithstanding, Poultney was by no means the first to suggest this device. In 1863–6 Archibald Sturrock fitted a considerable number of Great Northern goods engines with steam tenders. But steam cooled in the long pipe from boiler to rear cylinders, probably even partially condensed, boiler pressure was difficult to maintain, coal consumption was very heavy, and the arrangement did not long survive Sturrock's retirement in 1866. As for *River Mite*, it might have been anticipated that the superstructure was really too massive for the two lightly-built scale model chassis, which became distorted by the forces developed when the engine was working hard. Nevertheless, she ran for ten seasons before being condemned as unsafe and withdrawn in 1937, pending a rebuilding which was never undertaken.

At the end of September 1939 passenger carrying ceased, and *River Esk* and *River Irt* were laid up for the duration of the war. But narrow gauge trains still ran from Beckfoot to Murthwaite, hauled by a Muir-Hill tractor, and standard gauge trains thence to Ravenglass, to keep up the supply of ballast to the LMS. As maintenance was reduced to a minimum, the condition of the railway and the crushing plant steadily deteriorated. Concrete was cast at Murthwaite to replace rotted and broken sleepers and worn out granite hoppers, but even materials for concrete mixing were difficult to obtain. Nevertheless, the crusher was somehow kept in operation.

After the end of the war, tight controls were only very slowly relaxed, but it became possible to improve the track in time for passenger trains to begin running once again in the summer of 1946, hauled by the modified Muir-Hill tractor because neither of the two steam engines was in working

---

* Davies, W.J.K., *The Ravenglass & Eskdale Railway*, p. 80.

order. *River Irt* was overhauled in time for the 1947 season, but *River Esk* needed far more attention and did not become available until May 1952.

In the meantime, there had been major staff changes. Tom Jones succeeded Ted Wright as engineer in 1943. Gillon left at the beginning of 1946 and was succeeded as General Manager by Harry Hilton, who had joined the staff more than twenty years ealier. He faced an anxious future, for when Henry Lithgow, Sir Aubrey's original partner, died in November 1948, the Brocklebanks decided to sell the quarry and the railway. Both were acquired the following year by the Keswick Granite Company for £12,888, but as its interest was primarily to secure control of a competitor whose output, though small, was of superior quality, it had no intention of improving the plant or increasing production.

As it happened, Harry Hilton and his staff had almost completed arrangements for a gigantic blasting in the quarry, and when the charges were fired on 20 August 1949, 50,000 tons of stone were dislodged. Clearing, transporting and crushing this vast quantity kept the quarrymen and the Murthwaite plant busy until early in 1953. By then, Keswick Granite had become concerned at the condition of both the crushing plant and standard gauge railway and, as a report had stated that output would have to be increased by half to make the business viable, it decided to abandon all quarrying in Eskdale. The tourist railway was to be maintained, however, as until 1957 losses incurred in operating a subsidiary such as that could be set against the parent company's profits when assessing liability for corporation tax. But when that concession was withdrawn, Keswick Granite lost little time before putting the railway up for sale, in September 1958.

So for the second time in eighty years, the Ravenglass & Eskdale Railway lost its mineral traffic and faced a crisis.

It is not easy to sell a loss-making concern, not even one with a host of admirers and well-wishers, and Keswick Granite made it no easier by excluding from the proposed sale the only possible source of profit, Beckfoot Quarry, and by asking far too high a price, £22,500. However, they kept the trains running, and in August 1959 again advertised the railway for sale, but without naming a figure. This drew an offer of £4,000 for rails and sleepers only. But, aware of efforts to save the railway which were being led by Douglas Robinson, Clerk to the Muncaster Council, and backed by local people and enthusiasts, the Keswick company turned down that offer. Unfortunately, the encouraging noises showed no sign of generating solid support, and the Keswick company announced its intention to sell at auction as a whole or in lots on 10 August 1960. By this time, rather late in the day, supporters had organised a Ravenglass & Eskdale Preservation Society, and

The footplate of Northern Rock, built at Ravenglass in 1976.

to give the society more time to secure promises of cash, the auction was postponed for a month. Even so, the society was unable to offer more than about £5,000, clearly an inadequate sum. Fortunately there was a Birmingham stockbroker, Colin Gilbert, who had previously tried private negotiations without success, and he now gave the preservation society his support, enabling Douglas Robinson to continue bidding on their behalf until the railway was secured for £12,000. Help had also been offered by Sir Wavell Wakefield, a resident of Kendal, a distinguished former rugger player and by then a Member of Parliament and director of various public companies, though for the time being his help was not needed.

Colin Gilbert undertook to pay staff and maintenance costs through the following winter while the railway was without income. To establish his rights and those of the Preservation Society on a regular footing a new Ravenglass & Eskdale Railway Company was formed in March 1961, acknowledging Gilbert as Managing Director with effective control, and the Society as shareholders who could not be brought out without their consent. Society members promised voluntary labour, following the tradition well established on the Talyllyn and Festiniog Railways, which would include general maintenance and, in the summer season, provision of extra guards.

Harry Hilton had retired in 1959, having weathered thirteen clouded years, and Douglas Ferreira was appointed full-time General Manager. In the years that he has occupied the post, more than a quarter of a century, the railway has developed into a well-equipped, smartly-maintained and efficiently-operated concern, one that would have delighted Sir Aubrey, as would the achievement in 1964 of a small operating profit, the first for seventy years.

During the winter of 1960–1, Tom Jones was able to have the boilers of both steam locomotives re-tubed and the 0–4–4 tractor equipped with a new engine. Experiments with diesel traction began and, in 1962, a winter service was re-introduced, with one train in each direction worked by an internal combustion locomotive. Replacement of open carriages by fully-enclosed bogie coaches with large windows, far more suitable under the prevailing weather conditions, began. The most recent have been built to a standard design prepared at Ravenglass, 23ft. 9in. long and 3ft. 9½in. wide, fitted with aluminium bodies to reduce weight. However, as on fine days unenclosed vehicles are still very popular, new open bogie coaches, some roofed, have also been added. More than half the passenger carriages are fitted with the compressed air brakes now standard in Eskdale, and the remainder piped, so all trains are controlled by continuous brakes in compliance with statutory regulations.

By far the most exciting move was the decision of the Preservation Society to commission another steam locomotive, ordered from Clarkson of York, who obtained the boiler from the Bedford firm of Gower. The name *River Mite* was revived for this new 2–8–2, very similar in appearance and dimensions to *River Esk*, and in fact making use of the eight-coupled chassis from her steam tender. Like *River Esk*, the new engine incorporates side control of the pony truck, but limited radial movement of her rear axle gives her better riding qualities. *River Mite*'s journey from York to Ravenglass at the beginning of December 1966 was a spectacular piece of publicity, for she came all the way on a vehicle towed by a steam traction engine! Her livery is Indian Red with boiler bands edged bright red.

Ten years later, another steam locomotive was commissioned, a 2–6–2 named *Northern Rock*. This was designed by Ian Smith, who became the company's engineer when Tom Jones retired after just over fifty years devoted service. The locomotive fitting shop, which had been moved from Ravenglass to Murthwaite in 1931, was of course moved back again after the

The new *River Mite* completed in 1966. Driver Ron Clarke giving the final touches after overhaul and repainting and before her boiler inspection on 15 May 1987.

crushing plant was abandoned, and the new workshops at Ravenglass were so well equipped that *Northern Rock* was built there, apart from the boiler which was supplied by the Hunslet Engine Co. of Leeds. She has driving wheels of the same diameter (20in.) as those of the three early scale models, but cylinders larger than those of any other Eskdale engine, 6½in. diameter with a stroke of 9in. When she entered service in May 1976, she was probably the most powerful 15-inch gauge locomotive in Britain. In general build and appearance, with outside frames, a roomy cab, large dome and tall chimney, she altogether departed from the 'model' concept, and resembled the locomotives Ernest Twining had designed, and Trevor Guest had built, for Dudley Zoo and Fairbourne.

The dignified yet unpretentious appearance of Twining's locomotives had obviously influenced design at Ravenglass even earlier, for the ill-judged attempt to make *River Irt* resemble the scale models was reversed in 1972 when she was given chimney, dome and cab of reasonable dimensions. One more steam engine took to the Eskdale rails in 1982, an 0–4–0 well-tank built

River Irt, greatly improved after being given chimney, dome and cab of more suitable dimensions in 1972. At Dalegarth, 13 May 1987.

by Kerr Stuart for the 2ft. gauge railway at Dundee Gas Works, which had been a gift that no one at Ravenglass quite knew what to do with. One idea was to use it in forming a steam railcar, but the performance of *Sian* from Fairbourne, in September 1976 when the R & ER celebrated its centenary of passenger carrying, suggested that better use could be made of the gift. It was therefore re-gauged, given a trailing truck and side tanks (once *Ella*'s) and went into service as the 0–4–2 *Bonnie Dundee*.

One problem with small steam locomotives is what fuel to use. Coke gives out greater heat than coal and scarcely any smoke. Coal is cheaper, but when a coal burning engine is hard worked, it ejects half-burnt cinders which are strewn liberally over passengers in open carriages. Oil fuel was tried in the 1920s, but the fumes proved more objectionable than the cinders! However, when *River Esk* recently became due for an entirely new boiler, the first since 1923, it was decided to equip firebox and ashpan to burn coal on the Gas Producer Combustion System developed in the Argentine and South Africa, allowing low grade coal to be burnt and flying cinders eliminated. Contemporaneously the Festiniog Railway, where fuel oil was in use because of the danger of forest fires, similarly fitted one of its steam engines.

Great though the appeal of steam locomotives is to the general public and those who work with them, it must be remembered that it takes two hours in the morning to raise steam, and time again in the evening to clear the ashpan and smokebox ready for the next day's work. So, for special trains, sparse winter services and the first and last trips of the working day, the quick response of the diesel to the starter switch has advantages that cannot be ignored.

The Eskdale's early use of peculiar petrol power and the later Muir-Hill Fordsons made the introduction of diesels inevitable. The first was an

Shelagh of Eskdale, 4–6–4 diesel-hydraulic, completed by Severn-Lamb in 1969. At Ravenglass on 13 May 1987.

Silver Jubilee railcar set, constructed in stages between 1976 and 1984 with two powered vehicles and two trailers. At Ravenglass carriage shed. 13 May 1987.

Lady Wakefield, built at Ravenglass in 1978–80, Bo–Bo diesel-mechanical with 112 h.p. Perkins engine, leaving Ravenglass with the afternoon train on 17 May 1987.

Perkins, a much rebuilt machine; its origin was one of the Muir-Hill tractors of 1929, reconstructed about 1933 as the passenger tractor, re-engined with a 40 h.p. Perkins in 1975, and reconstructed in its present form in 1984 when it was officially named. Outside Ravenglass diesel shed, 15 May 1987.

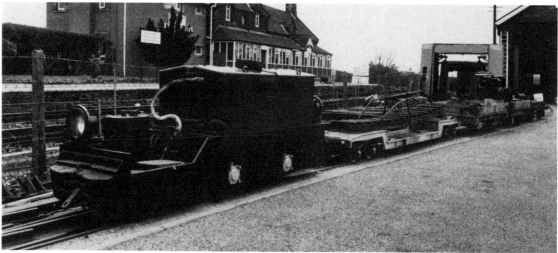

Greenbat, the battery electric locomotive with two 7½ h.p. motors, built by Greenwood & Batley of Leeds in 1957 for use on a 16-inch gauge railway in a fireclay mine, and acquired in 1982. Re-gauged by re-profiling the wheels, it has proved very useful for duties at Ravenglass. It is seen here on a works train, 11 May 1988.

attractive Bo-Bo diesel-hydraulic named *Royal Anchor*, after the Hampshire pub where it had been built by an amateur engineer in 1956. Although trials on the Romney Hythe & Dymchurch Railway had not been satisfactory, further trials in Eskdale in 1961 showed that its ability to haul a light load of six covered four-wheeled carriages made it worth having. In 1955, Tom Jones, looking ahead, began construction of a 4–6–4 diesel-hydraulic to incorporate a 40 h.p. Fordson engine and some parts of *Ella*, but work on this was interrupted by the decision of the Keswick Granite Co. to withdraw from Eskdale. In 1967, however, the parts were sent to Severn-Lamb Ltd. at Stratford-on-Avon, where the locomotive was completed with two bogies and a diesel having hydraulic transmission. The body was provided with a cab at each end, so *Shelagh of Eskdale*, delivered in 1969, was a handsome symmetrical machine. Ten years later, she was improved by substitution of a 112 h.p. Perkins diesel in place of the Ford engine first fitted, and her livery changed from blue to mid-green below and light green above, with bright red coupling rods and balance weights.

Next came a single diesel railcar, which grew into a four-car set composed of two powered vehicles and two trailers, fitted throughout with power control. Launched in 1977 and named *Silver Jubilee*, this replaced *Royal Anchor* and her light train. Apart from its work at home, it was particularly successful in operating the branch-line service at the Liverpool International Garden Festival in 1984. A Bo-Bo diesel-mechanical locomotive was designed and built at Ravenglass in 1978–80, a powerful machine fitted with a 112 h.p. Perkins engine driving through a gearbox; *Lady Wakefield* follows the pattern of General Motors main-line locomotives, in having the engine under a large bonnet behind a single cab. Her livery is maroon, lined bright red and grey, and she rides very smoothly. Another Bo-Bo diesel, justly named *Perkins*, was rebuilt in 1984 from the Muir-Hill passenger tractor; a 40 h.p. diesel-mechanical of conventional appearance, she hauls works trains and has been painted bright yellow with 'zebra' markings on the buffer beams as a warning to track maintenance men. There are other power units; perhaps the most intriguing is the diminutive *Greenbat*, a battery electric locomotive built by Greenwood & Batley of Leeds in 1957 for a fireclay mine near Sheffield and acquired in 1982 after closure of the mine. Suitably painted dark green, it has proved very useful for shunting duties in Ravenglass yard.

Locomotives are the show-pieces of any railway, but way and works – track, signalling and structures – must be of a standard to give travellers a safe and smooth ride and provide them with shelter (and refreshment) at the principal stations. When the new Ravenglass & Eskdale Railway Company

Ravenglass station as remodelled yet again, in 1966–7 with two main platforms, a bay for short trains (on the left) and a footbridge. The canopies from the Furness Railway station at Millom were added in 1972–3.

Ravenglass signal box and trackwork at the exit from the station, both part of the 1966–7 reconstruction.

was formed in 1961, weeds were flourishing and rails corroded after years of neglect. Weeds were dealt with by volunteers and chemicals, the ballast once supplied by the crushing plant was plentiful and in good condition, but new rails were necessary in some places and desirable throughout, so a long-term programme of relaying was started in 1963, with volunteers helping the trained permanent way gang. Rails weighing 35lb. per yard in 30ft. lengths replaced the previous 25lb. or 30lb. rails laid in the twenties, and from 1967 onwards these were spiked to new sleepers of Australian Jarrah wood.

Abandonment of tracks at Murthwaite left a passing loop at Irton Road only, 4⅛ miles from Ravenglass, not enough to enable a satisfactory service to be run for the burgeoning tourist traffic, so in 1976 two more were provided, at Miteside (1¾ miles) and Fisherground (5¼ miles), enabling trains to be despatched every twenty minutes if need be. A major civil engineering work had been undertaken at Hollinghead (5⅞ miles) to eliminate the reverse curves which had taken the 1875 line round a rocky bluff. Here, a cutting 400ft. long and up to 12ft. deep was blasted through granite or dug through soil at the personal expense of Colin Gilbert, whose name was given to it at the formal opening in March 1964.

Eskdale Green station, now known simply as The Green, was reconstructed on a slightly different site by members of the Preservation Society, with a car-park on the old site next to the road bridge. Ravenglass station was rebuilt yet again during the winter of 1966–7, when a new platform was added with a bay on the outer face, useful for short trains. Old and new platforms have canopies salvaged from the Furness Railway station at Millom, and are linked by a lattice iron footbridge spanning the three tracks converging on the turntable. Pointwork was simplified by laying a scissors crossover, and control of all points was concentrated in a 29-lever ex-BR frame housed in a signal box of traditional design. A four-road carriage shed was completed in 1967.

The train service on a railway largely dependent on tourists of course varies greatly according to the season of the year. In Eskdale, there is at least one train a day in each direction, even on Sundays in mid-winter, and this gradually increases to a maximum of fourteen during the summer peak, thereafter tailing off from early September to seven, five, two, one. Twenty years ago, there were never more than seven, and way back in 1924, only six. But in the early days, relief trains often had to supplement those shown in the timetable, and these and the special trains arranged for large parties, often at short notice, taxed the capacity of the line when there was only one passing loop – there is a well-known photograph showing two trains in each direction being worked past one another at Irton Road in the 1960s.

Interior of Ravenglass signal box, equipped with a 29-lever ex-BR frame, nearly all of which are used. Behind Graham Withers, signalman and controller, is the glass screen dividing off the controller's sanctum. 14 May 1987.

The new erecting shop in what was once the Furness Railway's goods warehouse at Ravenglass. The boiler of *River Esk* is seen on the right during overhaul of the locomotive in May 1988.

Timetables of the Mitchell era show that trains sometimes also crossed in the loop at Murthwaite, and even at Eskdale Green by shunting one into a siding. But although at busy times pilotmen rode on trains to and from the crossing place, traffic control was rudimentary and extra trains were despatched on the time interval system used in the very early days of railways, one fraught with danger should delay arise from natural causes or mechanical failure. More effective regulation of traffic became possible after a private telephone line was installed between Ravenglass and Irton Road, enabling the arrival or despatch of each train to be reported and special instructions given if necessary. Single line operation by train staff and ticket was introduced in 1975 on either side of Irton Road, providing secure operation for following trains because the driver of each except the last (which carried the staff) had to be shown the staff and given a ticket authorising him to proceed once the previous train had cleared the section. But, when the new passing loops came into use in 1976, dividing the line into four sections, this system caused too much delay for smooth operation of the intensive summer service.

It was superseded by an advanced method of control modelled on European experience in operating rural single tracks, but never previously used in Britain. It depends on radio contact between a controller at Ravenglass and the driver of each locomotive out on the line. All messages passing between controller and driver are repeated verbally and recorded on tape, the driver identifying himself by the code word formed from the name of the railway and the train number, e.g. RANDER 9. All movement is marked on a graph by the controller, first by a pencil line for every train scheduled to run that day, then by a horizontal red line indicating that he has given the driver authority to proceed through a particular section. The driver is given a sheet of written instructions telling him in which loop or loops he is to pass another train, and where to look out for men maintaining the track. Nearing the passing loop at the end of the section, the driver reports his approach, awaits permission to proceed beyond the loop and, when inside, reports that his last vehicle is clear of the points, whereupon the controller draws a green line covering, or lying close to, the pencilled path, depending on punctuality.

As it is possible to run a train every twenty minutes, specials can be arranged at short notice, the controller marking a suitable path on his graph and advising all concerned by radio. In case of accident, the driver will at once report its position and nature, and if he has been incapacitated, his whereabouts will soon be known from his failure to contact RANDER BASE from the next reporting point. Should radio reception be poor or fail

The Flower of the Forest, a free-lance interpretation of a street tramway locomotive built for Ian Fraser, waits in Miteside loop during her test run on 15 May 1987 for *Northern Rock* to pass with the 1.20 p.m. from Dalegarth.

altogether, the driver makes use of the locked telephone cabinet provided at each loop and station.

The system was approved by the Railway Inspectorate of the Ministry of Transport, who brought it to the notice of British Rail, and after their signal engineers had visited Ravenglass, a long single-track branch in Scotland was equipped experimentally, successful operation resulting in adoption elsewhere.

Not only have Ravenglass signal engineers advised other railways on radio control and planned installations for them, but their mechanical engineers have undertaken locomotive repairs and new construction for other narrow gauge railways and private owners. A delightful example is *The Flower of the Forest* completed in May 1987 for Ian Fraser of Arbroath, a free-lance interpretation of a street tramway locomotive such as was used from the 1870s until the introduction of electric traction, with all moving parts concealed from other road users. *The Flower* has a vertical boiler, single cylinder and flywheel, and two axles coupled by chains.★

★ Recently, a tourist railway in Japan has placed an order for Ravenglass to build another *Northern Rock*, *Kita no Iwa* in Japanese, for delivery in 1990.

Northern Rock taking water at the Fisherground tank.

Northern Rock gathering way from Dalegarth station as she crosses the Whillan Beck.

'Ratty', the nickname of the railway thought to have been derived from the Mr Ratcliffe who was in charge of construction in 1873–5, is an exceptionally friendly concern. As with other minor railways of today, several of the staff have come to it from British Rail or other occupations, the attraction of more personal management outweighing a lower income. Graham Withers, controller and signalman at Ravenglass, was a Western Region signalman; John McCullagh, booking clerk and editorial assistant to the Society, is a retired schoolmaster; Ron Clarke, formerly a BR driver, followed steam from Carnforth shed to Ravenglass. Ron's locomotive is *River Mite*, for each Eskdale driver normally keeps to one engine, which he learns to know intimately and in which he takes pride; *Northern Rock* is Trevor Stockton's, though another will drive her when Trevor stands in as controller in Graham's absence; Peter van Zeller, archivist and museum curator, has *River Esk*; George Staniforth's engine is *River Irt*.

As for the directorate, when Colin Gilbert died in 1968, his shareholding was acquired by Lord Wakefield of Kendal, the former Sir Wavell Wakefield, who took his place as managing director until his own death in 1983, since when Lady Wakefield and other members of his family have maintained the interest he had shown and the support he had given. So, with the help of a vigorous Preservation Society, Ratty's future seems assured.

CHAPTER FOUR

THE ROMNEY HYTHE & DYMCHURCH RAILWAY

A fter Count Louis Zborowski had been killed racing in October 1924, J.E.P. Howey, the friend who shared his interest in motor racing and 15-inch gauge railways, assumed responsibility for the two locomotives which the Count had ordered and which were already under construction in the Colchester Works of Davey Paxman. Howey had not revived his Staughton Manor Railway, so early in the summer of 1925 he had a magnificent scale model Pacific but no track on which to run it – nor would have unless he could turn fantasy into reality, the fantasy that he and the Count had dreamed up together. This was for no less than a double track miniature main line, over which trains would run at speed, carrying passengers between properly equipped stations according to a published timetable, and controlled by signalmen from signal boxes dividing the line into block sections.

Zborowski and Howey had the wealth that would enable them to do this, derived from landholdings in the two great cities of New York and Melbourne respectively, and now that Howey was alone, he determined that such a railway should be built, partly as a memorial to his friend. But where could a site be found for such an idyllic model railway? A site where a rich man's hobby would serve a public need? The two had been to Eskdale during the summer of 1924 and had fallen under the spell of its beauty; if they could buy the Ravenglass & Eskdale Railway, they would improve it,

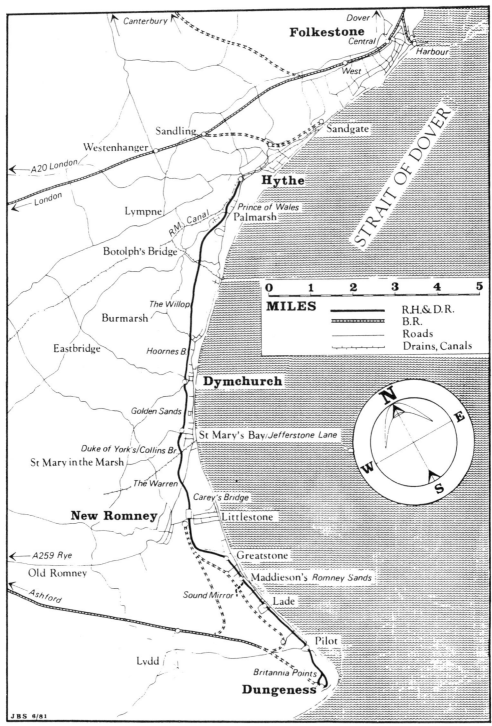

Canterbury

Dover

Folkestone
Central

Harbour

West

Sandling

Sandgate

Westenhanger

STRAIT OF DOVER

← A20 London

← London

Hythe

Lympne

Prince of Wales

R.M. Canal

Palmarsh

Botolph's Bridge

| 0 | 1 | 2 | 3 | 4 | 5 |

The Willop

MILES

R.H.&D.R.

Burmarsh

B.R.

Eastbridge

Hoornes B.

Roads

Drains, Canals

Dymchurch

N

Golden Sands

E

St Mary's Bay/Jefferstone Lane

Duke of York's/Collins Br.

St Mary in the Marsh

W

The Warren

S

Carey's Bridge

New Romney

Littlestone

← A259 Rye

Greatstone

Old Romney

Maddieson's Romney Sands

Ashford

Sound Mirror

Lade

Pilot

Lydd

Britannia Points

Dungeness

JBS 6/81

Map of the Romney Hythe & Dymchurch Railway (*J.B. Snell.*)

Green Goddess on test in Eskdale, J.E.P. Howey driving, June 1925. Designed by Henry Greenly and built by Davey Paxman & Co., Colchester. (*Ravenglass & Eskdale Railway: Mary Fair Collection.*)

drive under Hardknot and Wrynose passes and extend it to Ambleside. But the Eskdale railway's legal title to its land was questionable, and Sir Aubrey Brocklebank, who had only recently secured control, was not minded to sell. It was as well; the Eskdale line could never have satisfied their craving for speed, and the gradients and tunnelling involved in escaping from the dale head were obstacles likely to overwhelm even those enthusiastic amateur projectors. Quite apart from the difficulties, the thought of being confined within rolling stock of 15-inch gauge dimensions while passing through a long tunnel does not attract, even if the bore itself should be of far greater dimensions, and therefore more costly to drive.

Eskdale, however, was the only place where Howey's *Green Goddess* could be tested, and there she went in June 1925. Greenly had designed her as he had designed *River Esk*, on a scale of one-third full size instead of the one-quarter scale of *Sans Pareil, Colossus* and *Sir Aubrey Brocklebank*, giving a corresponding increase in power. *River Esk*, at that date still handicapped by the Lentz valves, had been built as a freight engine to work the stone traffic, *Green Goddess* with larger driving wheels for fast running. With driving wheels 25½in. diameter and cylinders 5¼in. × 8½in. she had no difficulty in outclassing the others. Photographs by Mary Fair show her with a respectable tail of wagons, a load of 34 tons compared with *River Esk*'s maximum of 29 tons. Greenly hoped for a speed of 40 mph, but the 35 mph she achieved easily was all that was practicable over the Eskdale curves and track. *Green Goddess* had been fitted with both Westinghouse and vacuum brakes, so useful trials were also made between air brakes and the vacuum brakes then in use on Eskdale stock.

Greenly was then commissioned to search for a site where gradients and curves would be minimal and holiday-makers plentiful. He found three: one in the west between Weston-super-Mare and Burnham-on-Sea, one in the south from Chichester to Selsey Bill, and the third across Romney Marsh in the south-east. As the first was already adequately served by the GWR, there was no public need that a miniature line would satisfy and every reason for the GWR to discourage one. The second had a railway of sorts, the Hundred of Manhood & Selsey Tramway, 8 miles long, one of the penurious light railways managed by Colonel H.F. Stephens of Tonbridge, made no more respectable by a recent change of name to West Sussex Railway. The acquisition of a ready-made track bed would have been an advantage to Howey, but the existing railway was standard gauge and as goods wagons passed to and from the Southern Railway at Chichester, the disadvantage of freight transhipment between standard and narrow gauge would outweigh any advantage passengers might gain from a better service; moreover, Stephens gave no encouragement.

That left Romney Marsh, that curious, featureless, flat but fascinating area gradually reclaimed from the sea through the centuries from Saxon times to our own, rich agricultural and pastoral land behind a coast speckled by holiday camps, inadequately served by branch lines of the Southern Railway. Sir Herbert Walker, General Manager of the Southern, had considered linking his New Romney and Hythe branches by a line through Dymchurch, by then the haunt of trippers rather than smugglers, but had decided against it for economic reasons. However, he realised that an attractive miniature railway might succeed where a standard gauge line would not, and therefore gave encouragement. For Greenly and Howey, the site was ideal: the main line could be laid for 8¼ miles with easy gradients and long straight reaches joined by gentle curves. There would have to be bridges across the Marsh sewers (or drainage channels), some of which were wide, but almost all the roads then carried very little traffic and could be crossed on the level without need for gates or signals. Freight traffic, coal inward, shingle outward, seemed a probability.

There was opposition from the local bus company, from farmers whose lands would be severed, from landowners who had their eyes on the fatter prices likely to be wrung from interested 'developers', and from the implacable Mayor of New Romney, a clever KC who wove a web of legal niceties in spite of the favourable opinion of the majority of the townsfolk. When a Light Railway Order was sought, all these – and some others – had their say at an inquiry lasting two days in January 1926. The principal weakness of the scheme was that the proposed line would not reach the Southern Railway at Hythe or Sandling Junction where the Hythe branch diverged from the London–Dover main line; both stood so much higher than the Marsh that first intentions had to be abandoned on account of the gradients involved. A further weakness was that the site chosen for the Hythe terminus was a good half-mile short of the town. Nevertheless, the Light Railway Order was granted in May.

Howey had already bought some of the land required, notably the site for the New Romney terminus and depot, and building had begun, much to the Mayor's fury! Through Francis Theakston, whose firm had supplied material for the 2ft. gauge light railways used on the Western Front, Greenly had acquired very cheaply a great deal of surplus War Department rail, much of it scarcely used; and where Howey had taken possession of the right of way, tracklaying, including pointwork manufactured by Theakston, had started. Both Howey and Greenly were living in bungalows erected on the site chosen for the railway's headquarters at New Romney.

There were two major engineering works, both within 1½ miles of this point. Where the route intersected the important Dover–Brighton coast road (A259) at The Warren, Howey had cheerfully proposed a level crossing, but fortunately Kent County Council insisted on a bridge, so the tracks dipped slightly to pass through two concrete spans; further on was the wide Marsh drainage channel known as the New Sewer, which could readily have been crossed (as it is now) by simple girders, but Howey, the model railway enthusiast on the grand scale, wanted something more spectacular, so Theakston provided steel truss girders with N-shaped ties through which the trains ran with impressive clatter.

Just beyond that point, at St Mary's Bay, the Duke of York (afterwards King George VI) had established a summer camp for boys drawn from homes and schools of very different standards, and it was his custom to join them annually. Like many others, he was attracted by Howey's enterprise and wished to see it during his 1926 visit. With a rush, the two bridges were completed in time and one track laid, so that on 5 August the Duke joined a train headed by the second of the Pacifics, *Northern Chief*, and rode on the

VISIT OF THE DUKE OF YORK, 5 AUGUST 1926.

Northern Chief, bedecked with Union Jacks, leaving New Romney, the Duke driving with Howey beside him and Gresley seated on the tender.

Northern Chief, with Howey in the driver's seat and a train of the first coaches to be delivered, waits for the Duke of York at the girder bridge across the New Sewer. Only one track was complete, and that only to a point a few yards beyond the bridge, thereafter known as the Duke of York's Bridge.

At New Romney engine shed. *Northern Chief* on the turntable; right of centre, Howey bringing the Duke forward; on the left, Gresley and Greenly standing talking by the edge of the turntable pit.
(Photographs on these pages by The Topical Press Agency.)

footplate, with Howey driving, from the girder bridge to New Romney, where he was shown round station and depot. Among the invited guests (a great many uninvited ones thronged New Romney station) was Nigel Gresley, Chief Mechanical Engineer of the London & North Eastern Railway, upon whose Pacifics Greenly had based the appearance of Howey's. On the return journey to what became known as the Duke of York's Bridge, Gresley sat perched on the tender while the Duke drove, with Howey beside him. It was a great day, and photographs taken by the Topical Press Agency, and published in the papers, gave the railway valuable advance publicity. Though too far away to have been a witness, I had followed closely those references to the building and equipment of the railway which had appeared in technical periodicals, and I was able to obtain a set of Topical's pictures, the originals of which the present New Romney management were glad to accept and use! There was also, of course, a set of six 'F. Moore' coloured postcards produced later by the Locomotive Publishing Company.

The model Pacifics were used to haul construction trains, but as they were scarcely better suited to this task than the Eskdale engines had been to handle

The Bug, designed by Roland Martens, built by Krauss of Munich in 1926 and used during construction of the railway. At New Romney after restoration.

the stone traffic, an 0–4–0 tank, with tender, was ordered from the German firm of Krauss in Munich in March 1926 and delivered the following August. Designed by Roland Martens as a scaled down version of his standard gauge shunter, the price was £340 in contrast to the £1,250 or so of Greenly's models. No. 4 proved useful, but neither her limited speed nor her appearance appealed to Howey, who rudely named her *The Bug* and, when she had served her turn, hid her away at the back of the locomotive shed until selling her in 1933. Surviving service on two pleasure lines and thirteen years of neglect, *The Bug* was eventually traced under a pile of scrap in a Belfast yard, rescued by W.H. McAlpine, brought home with honour in 1972, and subsequently repaired – one doubts whether Howey would have approved!

While the railway was still under construction, orders for more engines were placed with Davey Paxman: *Southern Maid*, No. 3, a sister for the initial two; Nos. 5 and 6, a pair of 4–8–2s to work heavy trains of ballast for supply to Kent County Council; and Nos. 7 and 8, a pair of 3-cylinder Pacifics to satisfy Howey's craving for a nearer approach to the Gresley prototype. As the 4–8–2s had no splashers on which to fix a nameplate, No. 5 was originally fitted with a straight plate reading *Man of Kent*, but Howey illogically insisted on a curved plate, and after running unnamed through 1927, No. 5 became *Hercules* on a crescent, her sister appropriately *Samson*; both were prone to derailment until Theakston supplied larger radius pointwork. The three cylinders of *Typhoon* and *Hurricane* were a luxury, producing two very speedy locomotives with voracious appetites and thirsts, but Greenly's valve gear was unreliable. *Typhoon*'s third cylinder was blanked off in 1935, but *Hurricane*, Howey's favourite engine, kept hers for two more years, until one day the gear seized up, causing chaos to the train service and a vindictive riposte by Howey who inflicted on her for a time the undignified name of *Bluebottle*!

All five new engines had been delivered by the summer of 1927 when the railway was officially opened on Saturday 16 July. The inaugural train was headed by the still nameless No. 5, and signalled away from Hythe by Earl Beauchamp, in his uniform as Lord Warden of the Cinque Ports, attended by Howey and General Sir Ivor Maxse (the shadowy Chairman of the Romney Hythe & Dymchurch Railway Company) in tails and toppers, while beside them walked Robert Hardie, the Traffic Manager (formerly the efficient superintendent of the Ravenglass & Eskdale), deferentially holding his hat in his hand. The watching crowd had overflowed from the platform to the trackside, led by a personage with a pipe in his mouth and smartly dressed in the 'plus fours' popular at that date.

So far, Greenly had designed everything – locomotives, rolling stock, signals, stations, bungalows – giving to the whole something of the air of a gigantic toy train set. The carriages were the least satisfactory part of the equipment; they were roofed but had open sides, and as the passengers were not to scale, the vehicles overtopped the engines, as in the Eskdale's early days. Some were fully fitted with vacuum brakes,★ others merely piped, but unfortunately they were four-wheelers, as on exhibition and garden railways of earlier years, unsuitable for the much higher speeds achieved across the Marsh, and still rough even when articulated in five-car and nine-car sets mounted on bogies except at the ends, where a single axle remained. The Marsh can be bleak and cold, not only in winter, and it was quickly realised that these vehicles were quite unsuitable for the intended winter running. So eight fully-enclosed bogie coaches with upholstered seats, steam-heating, electric light, carpeted floors and framed pictures above the seats, were built by the Clayton Wagon Company in 1928, splendid vehicles known as the

---

★ In 1927, vacuum was chosen in preference to air braking, and both *Green Goddess* and *Northern Chief* then lost the Westinghouse pump.

The opening of the railway on 16 July 1927. Earl Beauchamp, Lord Warden of the Cinque Ports, followed by Sir Ivor Maxse the Chairman, and Howey, both in morning dress with top hats, and, to the right, Robert Hardie, Traffic Manager, hat deferentially in hand.

The inaugural train, drawn by *Hercules*, leaving Hythe. Both photographs by the Topical Press Agency.

Forecourt and Clock Tower at New Romney station, little changed between 1926 and 1987.

Clayton Pullmans and so soundly constructed that they lasted more than forty years, their riding much improved in 1930 by fitting new bogies with roller-bearing axleboxes. One remains even yet, still retaining one upholstered compartment and, after long service in works trains, is now preserved pending restoration.

Meantime, Howey had decided to extend his railway 5½ miles from New Romney to Dungeness, a strange area of shingle built up by the prevailing south-westerly winds through thousands of years and still growing by some eight or twelve feet a year. There were not then the bungalows, nor the roads, and the fisherfolk walked the inhospitable shingle with boards called 'backstays' or 'baxters' fastened to their footwear, and used carts with wheels a foot wide. But towards the Ness there were The Pilot Inn, a lighthouse, a coastguard station and the terminus of a standard gauge branch line, for the old South Eastern Railway (and later the Southern) owned a large area, whence it drew ballast for its tracks, and in the shadow of the lighthouse had provided a timber platform to which it ran occasional passenger trains.

Why did Howey choose to extend the twin tracks to such a place? Did he appreciate the strange attraction of such wildness? Did he expect to encourage bird-watchers to ride to the famed landfall of rare migrants? Or did he foresee the spread along the coast of the dwellings which were already appearing at Greatstone? Consignments of fish were expected, and two low-side bogie wagons were built for it, though in fact these carried not fish, but baggage, bicycles, prams and push-chairs! Shingle ballast, however, was transported to Hythe; and, though this could not have been foreseen, men and materials were carried in the 1930s to a branch specially laid at the request of the army to serve the erection of huge concrete bowl-shaped structures, which were expected to magnify the sound of approaching enemy aircraft if war should break out.

Extension to Dungeness of course involved application for another Light Railway Order. For this, there was general support, especially from the coastguards and others with business at the Ness, and it was granted on 12 July 1928. Typically, Howey had jumped the gun, building and opening the first four miles to The Pilot Inn on 24 May. The remainder followed early in August. For half a mile from New Romney, the line rose from the level of the Marsh to reach the top of the bank which had been built in early medieval times to protect the harbour of the Cinque Port. Following this, it rounded Half Mile Curve leading towards the sea at Greatstone, and then climbed at 1 in 120 to the top of the coastal shingle bank. Beyond The Pilot Inn, there were ridges and deep furrows formed by the storms of many centuries, and across these the construction gang had to cut and fill to make a level path, for the most part laying the track direct on the shingle.

With considerable foresight, two bridges were built to carry roads where building was about to be undertaken, but many of the rough tracks and footpaths which then crossed the line on the level have since developed into proper roads, creating problems with motor traffic. Nearing The Britannia Inn, serving an intriguing colony of bungalows, many of which have sprouted from a kernel of old railway carriages of uncertain date and origin, the two running lines diverged to form a balloon-shaped loop, with the station at its head by the lighthouse and a length of double track so that two trains could be received and subsequently despatched in turn without reversal.

The station building was a substantial brick structure (it needed to be in such an exposed spot) which included a restaurant. Howey was averse to

Dungeness station in its original somewhat stark condition. 8 May 1949.

catering and had sold the restaurant alongside Hythe station, but at Dungeness there was no escape from retention of such a welcome and profitable facility. It serves, as it should, excellent locally-caught fish.

The most exacting and difficult work on the extension was to provide through lines at New Romney station. The terminus abutted on the road leading to Littlestone and the coast, and the existing tracks were too low for them to be extended across the road on the level – which was just as well – and too high to be taken under it. So the Dungeness lines had to dip, destroying some of the original work as they did so, and pass under the road through twin tunnels. The one platform for which there was space in a cramped train shed between what remained of the terminus and a retaining wall,★ was used by the Down trains from Hythe to Dungeness, and a platform for Up trains could only be provided on the far side of the tunnels. This proved so inconvenient for both passengers and staff that it was soon abandoned; instead, a very short platform was built in the open on the Hythe side of the overall roof, but it was so short that the tail of any train along-side it was under that roof and hemmed in by the retaining wall, with the result that passengers could only enter the rear coaches by crossing the Down line. This awkward and somewhat perilous arrangement lasted until

★ The retaining wall had been built to support a high-level line and goods shed in the expectation that freight would be transhipped to and from wagons on a Southern Railway siding alongside.

New Romney station as rebuilt in 1973–4. The site of the original station of 1926 was to the left beyond the signal box, behind the present Down platform.

The Canadian design of the Pacifics built for the Dungeness extension. No. 9 *Winston Churchill* with Vanderbilt tender. (*George Barlow.*)

the mid-1960s, when the retaining wall, no longer of any significance, was removed and the platform extended. Finally, complete rebuilding was undertaken in 1973–4, providing three through tracks, a bay for trains to Hythe, and three sidings for coaching stock, all under cover.

Although by no means all trains ran through to Dungeness, an increase of 67 per cent in total length meant that more locomotives were needed. The intention was to build at New Romney two new ones, designed by Henry Greenly as one-third scale models of Canadian Pacific 4–6–2s, the far more generous North American loading gauge enabling them to be fitted with larger cabs which would give the Romney enginemen almost complete protection from rain and wind. Wheels and cylinders were supplied by Davey Paxman with the same dimensions as the five earlier Pacifics – coupled wheels 25½in. diameter, cylinders 5¼in. × 8½in; the boilers were manufactured by Krauss of Munich, having a pressure of 200lb. per sq. in., later reduced to 180lb. on all except *The Bug* (171lb.). With the help of a CPR photograph, designs were being worked out locally when, in Howey's absence in Australia, a violent quarrel broke out between the touchy Greenly and the New Romney management and engineers. Greenly destroyed the completed drawings, departed in dudgeon, and the two locomotives were eventually built in 1931 by the Yorkshire Engine Company, using the parts already made. Numbered 9 and 10, they were named *Dr Syn* and *Black Prince*, and equipped with cowcatchers and tenders of the American Vanderbilt type (with the bunker surmounting a circular tank) and a scoop to pick up water from track troughs Howey was then proposing to install at Greatstone. Unfortunately, this spectacular development was never undertaken, and large conventional tenders with increased water capacity subsequently replaced the Vanderbilts. The two were never given the powerful headlamp typical of American and Canadian locomotives, but No. 9 was equipped from the first with a chime whistle made in Boston, so distinctive that two other RH & D engines were later given them – as also, after Gresley had heard them, were the streamlined LNER Pacifics and 2–8–2 express engines.

In 1948, No. 9 was patriotically renamed *Winston Churchill*, but as it was unthinkable for a railway crossing Romney Marsh, that former warren of smugglers, not to have an engine bearing the name of Russell Thorndike's fictitious Vicar of Dymchurch, No. 10 later became *Dr Syn*. Apart from rescue of *The Bug* in 1972, only one more steam locomotive has been added to the Romney stud, in 1976, one of three designed by Roland Martens and built by Krupp of Essen in 1937 for an exhibition at Dusseldorf. All three came to England after a long period of idleness, the other two going to Alan

Southern Maid at New Romney on 21 April 1987, resplendent in the livery of the former South
Eastern & Chatham Railway.

No. 10, *Dr Syn*, as modified in 1987 with a taller chimney, copper-capped, and American-style
bell on the buffer beam, setting off from New Romney with a flurry of steam from the cylinder
drain cocks.

Instanter couplings and vacuum hoses between two coaches.

Bloom's Bressingham Steam Museum in Norfolk. With driving wheels 22¾in. diameter and large cylinders 6½in. × 10in., these rank with Eskdale's *Northern Rock* among the most powerful engines yet built for the 15-inch gauge. Clearly, Martens had in mind the splendid Pacifics designed by Dr R.P. Wagner for the Deutsche Reichsbahn during the inter-war years. Fitted with an elegant chimney instead of a stove-pipe, Romney's No. 11 has the Reichsbahn livery of black boiler and bright red wheels, motion and buffer beams. Given the discarded name of *Black Prince*, she is a handsome and impressive little machine.

Livery of most locomotives has changed from time to time: that of *Green Goddess* is obviously immutable, and so is the blue of *Hurricane*, the colour she bore when so frequently driven by Captain Howey himself. *Hercules, Samson* and *Winston Churchill* are red, the latter in the pleasant subdued shade used by the one-time Furness Railway; *Samson* in Metropolitan style. *Northern Chief, Typhoon* and *The Bug* are green; *Southern Maid*, which has sported a great variety of colours in her time, including Brighton umber, has recently been repainted in the livery of the former South Eastern & Chatham

Railway, a darker green, elaborately lined out, and with a polished brass dome. *Dr Syn* is black, set off by a copper-capped chimney and a tender white-lettered in full 'Romney Hythe & Dymchurch', whereas other tenders bear the initials RHDR and the company's crest.

Each Romney engineman normally has his own engine (as do the Eskdale drivers), and although this means that when he has a day off his engine probably stands idle, it is considered well worthwhile, as he gets to know it intimately, his hand reaching automatically to the position of this or that control, his ear sensitive to any variation in the usual sounds, his pride in her shown by the cleaning rag and oilcan he uses at a stop of any length.

Unlike most narrow gauge railways, but true to the 'model' concept, Romney stock is fitted with side buffers. Locomotives have miniature screw couplings, coaches three-link couplings of the Instanter type introduced by the GWR for vacuum-fitted freight wagons, quicker to couple or uncouple, and having the middle link designed so that it can be used in either of two positions: to couple the vehicles loosely, or to draw their buffers together to avoid snatch on starting and clash when the brakes are applied. Instanter couplings and vacuum brakes ensure a smooth ride on the Romney line.

When war broke out on 3 September 1939, RH & D running was cut back, and in the early months of 1940 public services ceased altogether. But from the start, the camp at St Mary's Bay had been occupied by troops instead of boys, and Howey generously placed the railway at their service, running troop trains from Hythe as required. After France surrendered in June and the south-east coast stood in the front line against air attack and probable invasion, the railway took on a new and unexpected role, transporting materials for building block houses, gun emplacements, mazes of barbed wire on the beaches and forests of interlaced steel tubing below the tide line. There is a nice story that some civil servant at the War Office, studying the map of coastal railways, saw what he thought was an ideal stretch for patrol by an armoured train, and forthwith ordered one to be provided, ignorant that it was of such narrow gauge that recoil of a heavy gun would knock it off the rails! This may or may not have been the case, but certainly two railway-minded officers of the Somerset Light Infantry, a territorial regiment which had been sent to construct the defence works, realised the value of even so small a railway. The outcome was that the Somersets commandeered it, used it for local transport, and gave it the armoured train. *Hercules* was sent to Ashford Works and emerged with boiler and cylinders encased in steel plates which gave her very much the appearance of an illustration in a Meccano instruction book. With her, and also encased in steel plates, came two of the massive all-steel bogie wagons

The armoured train: *Hercules* encased in steel plates with former Ravenglass & Eskdale Railway all-steel bogie wagons. (*Imperial War Museum.*)

built for the Eskdale stone traffic and sold to Howey when standard gauge was laid to the Murthwaite crushing plant in 1929; each carried a Lewis gun and an anti-tank rifle, the latter later replaced by a Bofors. The train was kept, *Hercules* with steam up, in a special siding near Dymchurch under an elaborate camouflage creation.

The railway received plenty of attention from enemy aircraft, and damage was done to buildings, track and rolling stock, especially at New Romney, but the armoured train was never hit and the crew claimed the destruction of a German raider. The Somersets were followed by other units, some of which treated the railway with scant respect, needlessly adding their own to enemy destruction, until in 1941 it was at last taken properly in hand, repaired and maintained by the Railway Operating Division of the Royal Engineers.

There was still war work for the railway when plans for invasion had changed direction. One of the major problems to be solved was how to supply a mechanised army on hostile shores with petrol and oil. The solution evolved was to coil steel tubing on drums of very large diameter which would be towed across the Channel, unreeling as they went. Dungeness was one of several sites from which PLUTO – Pipe Line Under The Ocean – was to be launched. Pipes brought by the Southern Railway branch line were welded into great lengths on the light railway's New Romney platforms, and underframes were stripped of coach bodies to carry those lengths to Dungeness, distorting the shingle-ballasted track as the trains passed. But a quicker method was for caterpillar-tracked vehicles to drag the pipes across the shingle, effectively destroying the Romney's permanent way as they went.

So when the railway was restored to Howey's hands in July 1945, there was a vast amount of reconstruction to be undertaken before passenger trains could begin to run once again. Howey appointed Terence Holder, an old friend and son of an older friend, as manager with a salary of £500 a year and an expense allowance of £250. Labour was scarce until the troops were demobilised, but Holder was able to form permanent way gangs from un-repatriated prisoners of war, who tackled the overgrown, but little damaged, track between Hythe and New Romney and succeeded in making it ready for traffic by 1 March 1946.

Far heavier work was involved in restoring the wrecked Dungeness extension, and because even usable second-hand rails – let alone new ones – were unobtainable because of prior claims and strict government control, it was decided to use what serviceable rails remained in relaying it as a single track. This was completed as far as Maddieson's Holiday Camp at Romney

Sands, beyond Greatstone, by midsummer 1946, and to Dungeness early in 1947, an occasion celebrated – and publicised – by a visit of the comedians Laurel and Hardy.

Although all the locomotives had suffered more or less from disuse and neglect, enough were made fit to handle traffic while four were overhauled at Ashford Works in 1946–7 through the kindly cooperation of the Southern Railway, and *Samson* was rebuilt by a Brighton firm. This sufficed until the ageing boilers needed replacing. Between 1956 and 1964, each engine in turn was fitted with a new boiler of a standard design, superheated. Most also received new and larger tenders.

It was far harder to find serviceable rolling stock as so much had been wholly or partially destroyed by PLUTO, and the shortage was exacerbated by the unexpected crowds that turned up as soon as the railway re-opened, eager for an outing after the drab years of wartime and intrigued to see the tiny railway which had been patrolled by an armoured train. There were the Clayton Pullmans, but of the fifty-four comfortable saloons built by Hythe Cabinet Works in 1934–6, twenty-one had been stripped. Makeshift seating was all that could be provided quickly. Toast-racks were put on the stripped frames; flimsy saloon bodies with longitudinal seats on the five remaining Ravenglass hopper wagons. Three ancient Heywood bogie coaches came with the complete equipment of the Eaton Hall railway when the Duke of Westminster dismantled it in 1947. Some of this motley collection lasted far longer than intended, the last of the open toast-racks, for example, as late as 1979. Surprisingly, use of these potentially lethal carriages resulted in only one passenger being hurt through standing up as the train approached a bridge, after which they were covered by netting of chicken wire, and later by roofs of hardboard.

Nevertheless, difficulties were overcome, and the 1947 timetable included an enterprising innovation, no less than a non-stop run from Hythe to Dungeness daily during the high season, covering the 13½ miles in 45 minutes, averaging 18 mph in spite of frequent reductions of speed for the unprotected level crossings. The train was named *The Bluecoaster Limited*, and the title was displayed on a headboard carried by the engine and by roofboards on the coaches, which included a specially-built observation car astern. But it proved to be an extravagant publicity stunt, because it was sometimes lightly loaded and had always to be followed by a second train making the intermediate stops, so it was discontinued after the 1951 season. However, named trains do have charisma, so one ordinary train became *The Coronation Limited* in 1953 and *The Marshlander* later for a few years, and as part of the fiftieth anniversary celebrations in 1977 *The Golden Jubilee*

'The Bluecoaster Limited' shortly before setting off from Hythe on the non-stop run to Dungeness. George Barlow giving a final touch to *Green Goddess*. The coaches were some of those built by the Hythe Cabinet & Joinery Works in 1934–6.

re-introduced the non-stop run. Such a train, bearing the revived title of *The Marshlander*, is still run during the high season, but on Saturdays only. The regular present-day service is twelve trains each way in the peak holiday season, nine in the preceding and following weeks, and in March and October six on Saturdays and Sundays only. All but a few of these run the full distance between Hythe and Dungeness.

For a time during the early post-war years, the railway had what had always been hoped for, some freight traffic: aggregate for concrete, huge amounts of which were needed for the rebuilding that was in progress all over the country. Dungeness shingle was admirable for the purpose, and was already being taken before Howey joined with several partners to form the Romney Marsh Ballast Company and open pits beside the branch line built for the army before the war near Maddieson's Camp at Romney Sands. A crushing plant was set up, sixty tipping wagons acquired, and trains run to Hythe where the trucks were winched up a ramp and their contents tipped into bins to await collection by road vehicles. As far as possible, the ballast trains were run late in the day after the passenger services had ceased, and as the run to Hythe took eighty minutes and winching and unloading several hours, return with the empties was not completed until about midnight. To work the turn, *Hercules* was fitted with a powerful headlamp. But the standard tip wagons, re-gauged from 2ft. to 15in., were inherently unstable and accident-prone, liable to accompany the load into the hopper and subject to derailment so that following trucks piled themselves and their contents across the tracks. Once, the winch cable snapped and, gathering speed down the ramp, the wagons careered for nearly a mile, carrying the hapless guard with them. Nor was the traffic profitable, as Howey set the rate too low, so after little more than a year from November 1946, the run was cut back to a new unloading point at New Romney. This lasted until 1951, when the ballast company was sold and the new owners turned to road transport.

More profitable, and longer lasting, was the contract to carry perhaps a hundred of Maddieson's campers by special train to and from Hythe every Saturday during the summer. It would, of course, have been more convenient to carry them by road all the way between London and the camp, but Maddieson's application for a licence to do this was refused by the Road Traffic Commissioners. Nothing, however, could prevent the East Kent Road Car Company from running extra vehicles on their regular service from London to the coast and setting down the campers at Hythe Light Railway station as they passed.

Pre-war, the railway staff had been a small one, augmented by volunteers, especially drivers drawn from among the younger members of Howey's motor-racing coterie and the railway-minded sons of friends. Post-war, however, Terence Holder determined to recruit a greater number of permanent members. This was not difficult at first when young men released from the forces were eager to find employment, and he secured the services of a platelaying ganger, mechanics and carpenters for the work-shops, clerks for the booking offices and, above all, engine drivers. Two of the latter were outstanding – Peter Catt and George Barlow. Peter Catt had known and loved the railway in boyhood, joined it as soon as he was old enough and, when he had qualified, became driver of *Northern Chief*. Later, in 1964, he was appointed Manager, a position he filled successfully until sudden death at an early age in 1968. George Barlow had been a journalist, but he had a strong interest in railways and served through the war with the Railway Operating Division of the Royal Engineers, after which he decided he preferred steam to print and joined the Romney in 1947. *Green Goddess* became his regular engine for thirty years until he became Operating Manager. Four years later he reached retiring age, and since then he has lectured in many parts of the world about the railway he served and loves.

New Romney shed, 3 September 1987, young volunteers cleaning the Krupp Pacific, No. 11 *Black Prince*: Simon Oldfield, then 12 years old, on the ladder polishing the boiler, and his sister Emma, then 10, at work on the cab. Simon and Emma are well known to the RH & DR staff as enthusiastic helpers.

He it was who drove the railway's second Royal Train when the Queen, the Duke of Edinburgh, Prince Charles and Princess Anne travelled from New Romney to Hythe on 30 March 1957.

Minor railways, however, are seldom profitable, and can therefore pay only low salaries and wages. These may satisfy young enthusiasts for a time, or appeal to men who have passed retiring age but are glad to undertake work they will enjoy, still more to others who, weary of the 'rat race' and the trammels of distant bureaucratic management, have taken early retirement and need an active interest. Some may have been professional railwaymen; it is probable that all will share some knowledge of, and liking for, railway matters. Faced not only by low pay but also by long hours, and in the off-season set to work on whatever needs attention, they are sustained by the satisfaction of work well done with cherished artefacts, in the company of others of like mind, amid congenial surroundings – be those in North Wales, Cumbria or Kent.

In addition to the permanent staff, who now number about twenty-five, others have always been needed during the summer season, perhaps as many as thirty-five, usually students on vacation or retired folk glad of temporary employment. Furthermore, the railway has never lacked volunteers, who are worth encouraging if they are prepared to do a job properly, because they may, like Peter Catt, later on prove useful members of the permanent staff. Some of these volunteers are youngsters still at school who find pleasure in the inevitably grimy engine shed, cleaning and polishing the splendidly-maintained locomotives.

These locomotives and the railway on which they run were the creation of Howey's wealth alone, and this perhaps explains why he regarded it to the end of his days as his own to do what he liked with, taking liberties he should not have done. One of these was when he challenged Sir Henry Segrave, racing motorist and holder of a world speed record, to a race from Hythe to New Romney and, the public service cancelled, *Hurricane* and *Typhoon* tore along the parallel tracks regardless. He drove his 1914 Rolls-Royce, converted into a locomotive, at more than sixty miles an hour, and frequently travelled up and down the line at high speed on an improvised vehicle fitted with a motor-cycle engine, early one morning covering the 8¼ miles from New Romney to Hythe in 8¼ minutes. Of course, he himself had diced with death on the motor-racing circuits, but escapades such as these placed other lives in peril – fortunately, on the by-roads of the Marsh traffic was then still minimal.

Essentially, his outlook seems to have been that of a *model railway* enthusiast on the grand scale, rather than that of a man with a genuine interest in railways and all that they then meant; how else can one explain his insistence on 15-inch gauge model locomotives to pull out-of-scale vehicles? Or his contemptuous reference to the engines of the delightful and purposeful Lynton & Barnstaple Railway as 'Dreadful old things with long funnels'?★

Although his post-war income was not what it had formerly been, Howey was still a wealthy man, yet he and his wife practised economy to the point of meanness, both at home and in the running of the railway. Terence Holder, having re-established the railway on a secure footing and even made it profitable, was foolishly refused the increase in salary he deserved, and therefore resigned towards the end of 1948. A good manager was essential, but to the ex-army colonel who succeeded Holder, Howey paid only half as much. A staff pension scheme, instituted by this same Colonel Simpson during the Howeys' absence in Australia, was abolished on Mrs Howey's insistence after their return. Although the locomotives – his pets – were well

★ Quoted by J.B. Snell in *One Man's Railway*, p. 62.

maintained, inferior materials were used when coach bodies had to be replaced, and even new stock was fitted with wooden slatted seats instead of upholstery. Bridge girders, particularly the spectacular trusses of the Duke of York's Bridge, were allowed to deteriorate so badly for lack of regular repainting and maintenance that most of them eventually had to be condemned. Nor was the track in proper condition, as old rails from sidings were used as replacements on the main lines and re-laid on worn ex-British Railways sleepers that could not last long. Maintenance of buildings was also neglected. Decay spread with gathering momentum after Simpson resigned in 1952, and thereafter Howey, with waning energy, managed the railway himself – after his own fashion.

He died in September 1963, aged 76, and soon after, Mrs Howey, who was his sole legatee, sold the railway. Nominally, it was owned by a company, but of the 51,000 shares, just over 95 per cent were in Howey's name, and for £1 a share these were acquired in 1964 by two retired bankers. One was a sleeping partner; the other, S.H. Collins, moved into Howey's bungalow beside New Romney station, from which he kept a keen watch over what went on, but he put the actual management in the hands of Peter Catt, whom he liked and upon whose practical knowledge he knew he could rely.

The partners' intention was to restore the concern to good order and make it cover its costs, so that at a later date it might be profitably re-sold. But although they were aware of much that needed to be done, there was still more which was not readily visible, for example, the condition of the bridgework. An early improvement was to lengthen the New Romney platform used by trains arriving from Dungeness, another to equip that station with a cafeteria, an obvious need which had been steadily resisted by Howey; for this, Collins and Catt made most of the tables themselves. The best of the coach bodies they refurbished with patches, plastic wood and paint, banishing those in need of substantial repair to the back of a shed. But the report of a consulting engineer called in to examine the Duke of York's Bridge gave them all an unlooked for shock: it was necessary to replace it at once. This was done during the winter of 1967–8 with flanged girders upon the top of which long timbers were laid to carry the metals. The reconstruction was entirely satisfactory, but nevertheless the railway lost one of its distinctive features. Perhaps the consultant's report aroused doubt about the condition of steelwork hidden under the timbers of other bridges, for after Collins had received a personal shock through the sudden death of Peter Catt in the spring of 1968, he decided it was time to pull out.

A group of twenty-one, mostly local men, was then formed, and purchased the bulk of the shares, Collins himself retaining 4,670 and a directorship. The aim of the group was entirely commercial, but although they were led by a clever accountant, they failed to realise that the fares from the hordes of seasonal passengers had to cover so much more than the cost of coal and simple maintenance. However, bearing in mind the lesson taught by the Duke of York's Bridge (now renamed Collins Bridge), they did call for a survey of the six other bridges carrying the tracks over the Marsh sewers. When they received it, the report horrified them: the condition of one was actually dangerous; three others could be repaired at considerable expense, but even so their life would be short, and it would therefore be sounder policy to rebuild them completely as soon as possible. To some extent, Greenly's materials and methods were to blame, but the root cause was lack of maintenance. Only two were in passable condition, and it was evident that their girders, which could be seen from level crossings alongside, had been given some attention. All four in a bad state were soundly rebuilt during the three succeeding winters.

An experienced coachbuilder was engaged to take charge of carriage maintenance, but he soon found that the bodies of many of the vehicles laid aside by Collins and Catt were beyond repair, and that he would have to build entirely new ones to mount on the existing frames. A Chief Engineer was also appointed, and when the workshop had been rebuilt and equipped with machine tools, he was in a position to undertake heavy repairs and so avoid the expense of sending locomotives away to outside engineering firms.

A modest attempt was made to improve the state of the track, but extensive relaying was out of the question for the time being, and the few good second-hand 30lb. rails that were purchased sufficed for no more than 2½ miles.

All in all, the group had spent a great deal of money, but the prospects were not encouraging, for in spite of vigorous publicity, there seemed to be no hope of revenue ever covering expenditure; indeed, the cost of the work already undertaken had involved such heavy borrowing that the bank had become uneasy. What could be done to economise? Shortening the line was considered but, after close scrutiny, was rejected. So, also, was the idea of transfer elsewhere to a track bed abandoned by British Railways. Attempts to sell proved abortive, so total closure and sale of assets was threatened, although it was realised that such drastic action would raise howls of protest locally.

This it certainly did, but amid all the hubbub voices could be heard suggesting that enough people concerned to preserve a unique railway intact

In the workshop on 28 April 1988. *Black Prince* stripped down for overhaul.

A set of three 20-seater coaches of the 1972 pattern, built of hardwood and varnished.

would be found ready to provide capital, although it was unlikely that any dividend would be forthcoming for some years. Enquiries along these lines had already been made, but backers had been reluctant to make any overt move for fear of inflating the selling price. On the other hand, the vendors were eager to recoup their investment on the best terms obtainable, and the publicity they gave to their threat of closure was probably intended to bring matters to a head.

It had the desired effect! Richard North, director of an engineering firm, who had known the railway for some years – and driven its engines – was the prime mover. He was able to gain the support of W.H. McAlpine, widely known for his interest in railways and with ample means derived from the McAlpine contracting firm. With the help of his name and influence, thirty others agreed to subscribe interest-free loans of £1,000 or more each, and to join in forming a holding company; and, after hard bargaining, the new group acquired in 1972 all but 553 of the 51,000 shares at something over £2 a share. At a later stage the company 'went public', but although new shareholders provided a useful injection of cash, the amount raised was far less than had been hoped for – after all, the number of people prepared to subscribe not less than £100 with little likelihood of any return is strictly limited!

When the new owners examined the condition of their acquisition, they found only one satisfactory feature: the bridges had been made safe. Locomotives, coaches and track were still in need of a great deal of attention, and so also were most of the buildings, so the problem they faced was what to tackle first. They decided that carriages must take priority, because shortage of seats had resulted in prospective passengers being left behind. Of a total of seventy-nine coaches, the bodies of twenty-one had to be scrapped, but there were others that could be roughly patched, and underframes which could be fitted with new wheels, vacuum brake gear and toast-rack seats. There were also other frames which could be lengthened to seat twenty, instead of sixteen, in new bodies; as these were built of a hardwood and varnished, instead of being painted, they were reminiscent of the splendid teak coaches so long characteristic of the Great Northern and London & North Eastern railways. But alas! rising costs led to the adoption in 1976 of aluminium panels lined with plywood, cheaper to build and maintain. Although all seats were cushioned, none of the new bodies had the luxury of the Clayton Pullmans of 1928 or the comfort of those built in 1934–6 by Hythe Cabinet Works (whose interior fittings were greatly superior to their coachbuilding). A return to something exceptional was, however, achieved in 1977 when a Bar Car, 32ft. long, was built with seats for sixteen, electric

The Pullman Observation Buffet Car built in 1977 and named *Gladys* after Mrs Howey, at the rear of a Hythe–Dungeness train in New Romney station.

The frontage of Hythe station as rebuilt in 1972.

Dungeness station in October 1987, greatly improved by rendering and a white coating – compare with the illustration on p. 87.

light, gas heaters, and not only a bar counter, but also a cooker and a sink so that hot drinks and light refreshments could be served to passengers willing to pay a supplementary fare. For several years, this remarkable vehicle was painted in gaudy colours with blatant advertisements displaying the name of a sponsoring firm and their product, Courage Brewery being one. It looks much better now as *Gladys*, the Bar and Observation Car discreetly painted chocolate brown with Pullman crest.

As all this work on the coaching stock kept the railway's own workshops fully occupied, overhaul, and in some cases complete rebuilding, of locomotives had to be entrusted to outside firms, and eight were sent away in turn during the ten years up to 1981.

As for the buildings, all four of the principal stations needed attention. The new owners were as well aware as the public who used it that the Hythe terminus was a disgrace, remaining as Greenly had designed it in the mid-twenties with no covered accommodation for waiting passengers except on the platforms of the train shed. Facing the forecourt there was a primitive booking office with a veranda affording little shelter, and in the car-park the body of a superannuated standard gauge coach housed a shop selling books and souvenirs. As Hythe had always been used by a greater number of passengers than any other station on the line, improvement was long overdue. So in 1972 it was rebuilt with a proper frontage and an entrance leading into a concourse which has the booking office on one side and a shop on the other. At Dymchurch, headquarters of the famous armoured train, massive blast walls had been built to protect army personnel; these and Greenly's overall roof were removed, and additions made to the doll's house of a ticket office so that there is shelter under a veranda and space for a shop and tea bar. The Dungeness building was given a new floor and roof, and the walls were rendered to protect them from the weather, which mollified the previous stark appearance of the brickwork. The contemporary reconstruction of New Romney station has already been described.

Winter by winter since 1972, sections of track have been completely re-laid, using at first good second-hand rails and more recently new 45ft. lengths, all secured to new sleepers. But undoubtedly the greatest improve-

The locking frame in Hythe signal box, made by the Jackson Rigby
Engineering Co. at New Romney in the 1920s.

ment during the same period has been the introduction of efficient signalling. Howey had erected signal boxes at Hythe, Dymchurch and New Romney, and had equipped them with locking frames specially made by a local engineering firm with levers considerably shorter than those found on standard gauge railways; these controlled all points and semaphore signals. The Dymchurch box, provided in the expectation that some trains from New Romney would terminate there, and that a turntable, sidings and crossovers were therefore required, subsequently proved unnecessary, but the station office has always acted as a block post intermediate between the Hythe and New Romney signal boxes. Train movements between the three are authorised by telephone, only one train at a time being allowed to occupy a section on the Up or Down line. But there were no block indicators in the boxes to remind the signalman whether he had allowed the section to be occupied or not, and safe operation therefore depended on meticulous accuracy in the record made in the train register, identifying each train by the number of the locomotive and showing the time it entered and left the section. Except that Howey replaced the semaphores by colour light signals in the 1950s (some semaphores have been restored at Hythe station for the sake of appearance), the same system is still in operation.

The weakness is, of course, the dependence on the signalman recording the time of each movement, and the most serious accident in the history of the railway occurred in June 1963 because the Hythe signalman deliberately omitted to do this. He had despatched one train, but the engine was steaming badly and came to a halt on a curve little more than a mile from Hythe. After what he supposed to be a sufficient interval, the man assumed that it had passed out of the section and, without making any enquiry, sent away another train. It was a reversion to one of the worst features of early railway operation – despatch of trains on the time interval system. Rounding the curve, the driver of the second train saw the stalled one ahead, but although he immediately applied the brakes, he was unable to avoid collision. Twenty-two passengers had to be taken to hospital, and there was extensive damage to the rolling stock of both trains.

A less serious collision through disregard of the rules had occurred eleven years earlier at Dungeness, where the two halves of the circular loop unite at the Britannia Points to become the single track to New Romney. This section of line is worked on the 'staff and ticket' method, making it possible for one train to follow another to Dungeness, the driver of the first being *shown* the staff or tablet and authorised to proceed by possession of a token, the second carrying the tablet itself and allowed to go ahead on receipt of a telephone message that the first has reached Dungeness. There, the same process is repeated, the driver of the leading train not leaving the station until the second has arrived and he has seen the tablet. On this occasion, however, the driver was told to proceed as far as the Britannia Points where he would be shown the tablet carried by the incoming train; he was there first, forgot his instructions and went on his way. Fortunately, the track is visible for a long way ahead upon the shingle, giving both drivers time to reduce speed before the trains collided, and damage was restricted to the buffer beams of the two engines.

Once, in 1954, high wind caught a train on an exposed part of Half Mile Curve, blowing off the rails an unstable van which dragged *Hurcules* off in its turn; the wind laid both on their sides, but the coaches remained upright. On another occasion, in 1967, *Hercules* made a spectacular arrival at Hythe, crashing through the buffer stops and ending up in the station forecourt. Most accidents, however, have occurred on one or other of the thirteen unprotected level crossings, their frequency increasing as motor traffic multiplied until, according to John Snell, Managing Director since 1972, there was roughly one serious collision each year. The road vehicle generally got the worst of it, but in 1946 *Southern Maid* nearly ended up in a Marsh sewer after hitting a lorry, the driver of which lost his life, and the following year *Typhoon* was cast on her side after smashing a farm tractor stalled on an occupation crossing, fortunately without injury to those involved. The most distressing was in 1973 when some wanton youths stole a car, raced off at high speed regardless of other road users, and struck *Samson* crossing St Mary's Road, killing her driver.

This accident brought matters to a head, and with the cooperation of the local authorities, who paid about half the cost, and the approval of the Ministry of Transport, flashing warning lights were installed, first at the five crossings between Hythe and New Romney and later at the eight between there and Dungeness. The lights are actuated by track circuits triggered by an approaching train, and proof that they are working correctly is given to the driver by a flashing white light at the track side, in the absence of which he must stop his train before crossing the road. At Dymchurch, however, two crossings are so close together that a three-aspect colour light signal, operated by the station staff, has been provided to assure the driver of a non-stop train that both are clear. Installation of the warning lights has enabled the previous speed restriction of 5 mph to be raised to 15 mph.

There have been other signalling developments. The long single-track section, out and home between New Romney and Dungeness, has been divided by insertion of a passing loop and tablet exchange at Romney Sands (Maddieson's Camp). Far more important is the creation of a train control

Winston Churchill crossing Jefferstone Lane, the warning lights flashing. 3 September 1987.

office on New Romney station; a private telephone circuit linking it with signal boxes and stations has now been replaced by radio sets which enable the controller to communicate rapidly with other key points and individuals as well, and very soon it will also be possible for him to make contact with the driver of each locomotive out on the line. Every message is recorded on tape as it is spoken. The equipment for all these developments in signalling has been designed and installed by the railway's own staff.

Although a great deal of money has already been spent and the railway is now in excellent condition, there remains, as always, more to be done. But Kent is not now the popular holiday area it once was, and the 400,000 passengers who patronised the railway yearly in the immediate post-war period has fallen to around 200,000. This has caused much heart-burning and renewed consideration of closure or removal. But there are the holiday camps, and the local authorities recognise that Romney Rail is one of the local attractions. Their respect for it was no doubt enhanced when they were faced by the problem of transporting some 220 children daily from around Dymchurch to an enlarged secondary school at New Romney, and the railway, rather than the bus company, tendered successfully to do so. The service began in 1977 and has been maintained regularly during term time,

The diesel locomotive, No. 12 *John Southland*, built 1983, on the turntable at New Romney, now operated electrically. 31 October 1987.

The cab of *John Southland*. The driver's cushioned seat, seen in the bottom right-hand corner, is at floor level, so he is obliged to sit in an uncomfortable position with his legs stretched out in front of him. Eskdale's *Lady Wakefield* is better in this respect, as in front of the seat is a well in the floor for the driver's feet.

even through the hard winters of recent years when the long train of up to nineteen coaches has been moved by two steam locomotives, one at each end and the leader with a snow-plough. For normal winter operation, however, a diesel is far more convenient and economical, and after *Shelagh of Eskdale* had been borrowed in 1981 for a year, the Romney Company ordered its own. No. 12, delivered by the builders, TMA Engineering Ltd. of Birmingham, in 1983, is fitted with a 112 h.p. Perkins engine, and is powerful enough to haul the train alone, on the return journey propelling it under instructions from a driving trailer. A fine-looking machine, she is painted red with a broad horizontal band of lighter red between yellow borders, and bears the name of *John Southland* who founded the original Southland's School as far back as 1610. Her greater height, equal to that of the coaches, imparts a more impressive appearance to a train than do the over-topped steam engines – Ernest Twining won a trick with his 'Colonial' style locomotives which ran at Fairbourne and influenced design at Ravenglass, having taller chimneys and larger cabs than are possible on a scale model. Recent modifications to *Dr Syn* have had much the same effect.

Shelagh's appearance at Romney is only one example of a number of locomotive exchanges between the 15-inch gauge railways. Some have been made to provide comparative information, as when Eskdale's new diesel, *Lady Wakefield*, was tested at Romney before *Shelagh* was borrowed; and when *Northern Chief* was sent to Ravenglass in 1971 to find out whether superheating would show the same economy in coal consumption on the Ravenglass & Eskdale as it had done on the Romney. Other exchanges have been on festive occasions: in 1976 the Eskdale Centenary of Passenger Carrying was attended by *Dr Syn* from Romney and *Count Louis* and *Sian* from Fairbourne, as well as by *Black Prince*'s sister *Rosenkavalier* from Bressingham and the veterans *Little Giant* and *Blacolvesley*; while for the Paxman Jubilee in 1985, *River Esk*, the only Eskdale locomotive built at Colchester, came south to take part in a parade with the seven Romney engines from the same stable.

★   ★   ★

I came to Folkestone at the beginning of May 1949, and within the first week I visited Hythe station one afternoon and the next day travelled to and from Dungeness, on the way back spending several hours at New Romney station and depot. Later that summer, I joined *The Bluecoaster Limited* for the non-stop run to Dungeness. The railway was then in the good shape restored to it by Terence Holder and maintained by his successor Colonel

Simpson. Later visits, and there have been many over the years, revealed the spreading deterioration, most noticeable in the condition of the track as it gave increasingly rough rides. Certainly some improvement could be observed in the 1960s, but it is the 1972 group who have given the railway the thorough reconditioning it needed and, further, have added equipment and amenities beyond any considered necessary by Captain Howey.

The local authorities were sufficiently impressed by the operation of the school train to support the purchase of the new diesel locomotive. Let us hope that they can be persuaded to do more to ensure that Howey's railway will remain in Kent.

★   ★   ★

Speed along straight level tracks – alone of the narrow gauge railways, the Romney Hythe & Dymchurch Railway has that. It is a feature greatly appreciated by Eskdale drivers who have come south with a locomotive from time to time. As any reader will have realised, I admire Romney Rail greatly, but give me hills and running water and the varying speeds imposed by changing gradients and awkward curves beside the river, against a background of rock and mountain. Romney Marsh has its own peculiar fascination, but it cannot compare with the splendour of the Eskdale scenery.

CHAPTER FIVE

THE SAND HUTTON LIGHT RAILWAY

O f all the narrow gauge railways in Britain, the Sand Hutton must be one of the least known. Its life was very short, April 1922 to June 1932, a period when narrow gauge railways were not of interest to many. Its length was just under 6¾ miles, and as the countryside through which it ran, some seven miles to the north-east of the City of York, is very beautiful but not spectacular, the railway did not attract tourists as did the Talyllyn and Ravenglass & Eskdale, both of which were of much the same length.

It ran from Warthill station, on the York–Market Weighton–Beverley–Hull line of the North Eastern Railway, through the grounds of Sand Hutton Hall and beyond, to serve the farms on an estate in a prosperous agricultural and pastoral area.

The owner of the estate, Sir Robert Walker, fourth Baronet, was the heir of a family which had become influential in York and the East Riding during the nineteenth century. His great-grandfather, son of James Walker of Springhead, Hull, had been High Sheriff of the City of York in 1846 and was created first Baronet of Sand Hutton in 1868. The second Baronet was MP for Beverley 1859–65, and on the death of the third in 1900, his son Robert inherited some 7,000 acres, a source of great wealth.

He was ten years old and, like many of his contemporaries, fascinated by the glamour of the railways, then at the height of their appeal to young and old. Like other boys of his day, he acquired a model railway, but his wealth enabled him to develop this interest beyond the wildest dreams of most. As a teenager, he had an outdoor track with a swing bridge across the Sand

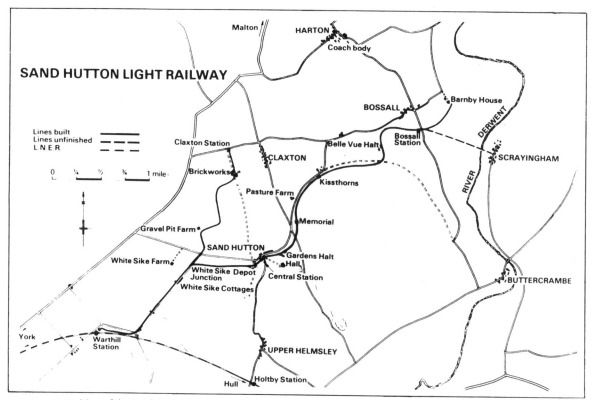

Map of the Sand Hutton Light Railway, drawn by Mike Swift and reproduced by permission of the Narrow Gauge Railway Society.

Hutton Hall drive. When he came down from Cambridge, he built a 15-inch gauge railway within the grounds and enjoyed himself driving a steam locomotive and giving rides to his friends.

He himself stated[*] that he 'began to experiment with a narrow-gauge railway of 15in.' in 1910, but not until the summer of 1912 could he have obtained, as he did, the first of Bassett-Lowke's Class 30 Atlantics. Named *Synolda* after his first wife, this fine engine was smartly finished with a polished brass dome and safety valve cover and a livery of dark green, lined white and black. With it came four of the firm's open four-wheeled carriages equipped with vacuum brakes, and in the estate workshops two more vehicles were built: a bogie saloon coach seating ten and a four-wheeled brake van. There were also one or more wagons.

In forming the railway, Sir Robert had the advice of Sir Arthur Heywood, and it was almost certainly through Sir Arthur's influence that Harry Wilde,

[*] Walker, Major Sir Robert, Bt., MA, 'The Sand Hutton Light Railway', *The Railway Magazine*, vol. 55, December 1924, p. 432.

Sir Robert Walker's 15-inch gauge garden railway in the grounds of Sand Hutton Hall. Sir Robert driving *Synolda*, the first of Bassett-Lowke's Class 30 Atlantics, completed in the summer of 1912. From a contemporary coloured postcard issued by the Locomotive Publishing Company.

The bogie coach built in the estate workshops, and later acquired by the Ravenglass & Eskdale Railway, where it was known as The Glass Coach. Photographed in Ravenglass Carriage Shed on 11 August 1924.

the Duke of Westminster's driver, came from Eaton Hall to give practical assistance in constructing it. When *Synolda* arrived, only 350 yards of track had been completed, but in a little over a year this had been extended to 1,245 yards from the Village station near the drive gates to Fishpond station, having threaded its way through a plantation, round behind the house, crossed a bridge over an arm of the pond, and run through a short tunnel. There was an engine and carriage shed at Garden station in the plantation, an embankment about 4ft. high, a cutting 6ft. deep through clay and another 5½ft. deep through rock. In places, there were gradients as steep as 1 in 70 and 1 in 60. Each of the three stations had a timber platform and a running round loop, but there was no turntable, so *Synolda* returned tender first from Fishpond. During a series of test runs the engine was driven by Cecil J. Allen, the expert recorder of train speeds who wrote for *The Railway Magazine*, and he timed a maximum speed of 23¼ mph. But there was a consensus of opinion that this was exceeded on the final trip, run tender first with the same load of 19 cwt., when Allen was unable to use his stop-watch because at that speed on such a narrow gauge he had to watch the track and the behaviour of a lively engine very closely.

Not only did this railway give pleasure to Sir Robert and his guests at the Hall. It was also in operation when fêtes and garden parties were held in the grounds, and it is said that the local children were given rides after attending Sunday school – which no doubt increased attendance as well as mothers' work on Monday wash-day!

So, in construction, working and maintenance of a miniature railway, Sir Robert and his invaluable engineer George Batty had plenty of experience before the outbreak of war in August 1914.

Sir Robert was no dilettante however. He took a keen interest in the management of his estate, which he increased to some 10,000 acres. Before he was twenty years old, his Sand Hutton Fire Brigade, equipped in those days with a horse-drawn, coal-fired Merryweather engine, served a wider area than his own estate and was capable of holding its own in competition with brigades from Yorkshire towns and cities. He encouraged his employees to join the Territorials, and himself held a commission as Major in the Coldstream Guards with which he served on the Continent until early in 1915, when he was sent by the Imperial General Staff to train New Zealand troops. His first wife went with him, and George Batty followed later.

Soon after their return home in 1919, he determined to extend his 15- inch gauge line to serve the estate, its farms, and a brickworks at Claxton, and to connect with the North Eastern Railway at Warthill, for at that date light railways offered the most economical and convenient means of transport between main-line stations and the surrounding countryside. He himself claimed, in an article published in *The Railway Magazine*,[*] that a farmer dependent on road transport to and from a railway station four miles away would have to employ one man and a horse and cart for almost a day in order to load a ton of produce at the farm, lead it to the railhead, tranship it to a railway wagon and make his way back, and that to despatch five tons would cost about 30s., whereas a light railway would relieve his men of all the labour except the initial loading and charge no more than 15s. Inward freight would reach the farm not only more cheaply, but several days earlier, saving the time taken up by postal notification from the station that a load awaited collection, as the light railway would take charge of it at once and advise him when it had reached the nearest siding.

To construct a railway which would cross public roads and carry passengers as well as freight, a Light Railway Order was necessary. Sir Robert applied for one as early as November 1919, and it was granted in January 1920 and confirmed by the Ministry of Transport on 1 May. The main line was to run from Warthill to Sand Hutton village, Kissthorns, Bossall and across the River Derwent to Scrayingham, just over 5¼ miles. There were to be two substantial branches, one nearly 1½ miles long from White Sike Junction to Claxton Brickworks and Claxton Depot beside a main road, and the other nearly half a mile long from Bossall to the outskirts of Barnby House, the residence of one of the directors, where there would be public sidings for the use of neighbouring farmers. Minor branches, really little more than sidings, would be laid to the Hall, a gravel pit and three farms. Altogether, the intended length was 7½ miles. There was no requirement to fence the line, but at level crossings and intersections of field boundaries, cattle-guards were to be provided; nor was any signalling mandatory unless trains were to pass one another, in which case a home signal and, if necessary, a distant signal, was to be erected and interlocked with the points of the loop. At stations or halts, neither platforms nor shelters needed to be provided. The capital of £25,000 (with power to borrow £8,000 on mortgage) would be subscribed by Sir Robert Walker and the Trustees of the property.

Construction began as soon as the Light Railway Order had been confirmed, and by the end of 1920 had reached both Sand Hutton and Claxton Brickworks, *Synolda* happily managing construction trains over gradients that were mostly easy with only short stretches of 1 in 100.

---

[*] Walker, Major Sir Robert, Bt., MA, 'Light Railways and Agriculture', *The Railway Magazine*, vol. 54, May 1924, pp. 361–7.

Beyond Sand Hutton, however, the route was undulating, with three banks of 1 in 80, each about half a mile long, and a final 1 in 65 on the branch to Barnby House.

These gradients must have raised doubts whether *Synolda* was suitable for hauling freight as well as passenger trains beyond Sand Hutton. Certainly they were not as stiff as those on the Ravenglass & Eskdale Railway, but on that line the bulk of the goods traffic was then being handled by the rugged Heywood engines, not the scale models. In any case, several more locomotives would have to be obtained in order to work the main line and the brickworks branch, and to cover the days when engines were withdrawn for servicing, such as washing out the boiler about once a week.

There is no record of how Sir Robert intended to increase his 15-inch gauge locomotive stock. In 1919, Henry Greenly designed a 2–8–4 single-boiler Fairlie articulated engine which may very well have been intended for Sand Hutton, as his drawing was found among railway archives in York where it might have been sent by Sir Robert for examination by North Eastern engineers. But a stud of such complex machines would have been very expensive, and even if Greenly had produced a powerful 2–8–2 as he did for Ravenglass in 1923, the cost of several would have been great. However, that point was never reached, for in December 1920 locomotives and rolling stock used in Deptford Meat Depot were advertised for sale. The depot had been established some twenty years earlier, but had been taken over by the War Department at a critical time during the First World War and equipped with an 18-inch gauge railway, a large number of small wagons and twelve 0–4–0 steam locomotives. Government surplus was always a bargain, and although use of it would mean re-laying the completed part with heavier rails 3in. further apart, Sir Robert decided the opportunity was not to be missed, and bought some of the engines and wagons.

Robert Hudson Limited, the Leeds light railway specialists, supplied about ten miles of new track: flat-bottomed rails weighing 20lb. per yard instead of 16lb. as used on the 15-inch gauge at Sand Hutton; and simple pointwork with weighted levers thrown over by hand. The rails were spiked to wooden sleepers, mostly from the wealth of trees on the estate, ballasted with gravel or ashes. Re-laying from Warthill to Sand Hutton and on the Claxton branch, and new construction as far as Kissthorns, was completed in time for freight trains to begin running in April 1922, but the cost was about £4,400 per mile, double what it would have been before 1914, and Sir Robert had then to call a halt. Work began again in May 1923 and was completed to Bossall and Barnby House in December. Only a little over half a mile remained to reach Scrayingham, but this included the bridge across the Derwent and its towing-path, which the Light Railway Order had specified must consist of a single span not less than 15ft. above the summer level of the river, and must be built without interrupting navigation. Unlike the rest of the railway, which was constructed with local labour, a bridge with a span of 100ft. would have to be erected by engineering contractors, and although late in 1924 Sir Robert still expected the extension to be built, he and his fellow directors eventually decided that the expense, estimated at £1,000, was not justified, so Scrayingham was never reached.

Association with the North Eastern Railway was close. Of course that great railway company would benefit from any increase in the traffic handed over to them at Warthill, and their officers may have felt that it was worth encouraging the Sand Hutton scheme because success might well result in promotion of other light railways intended to boost agricultural production. But a hard-headed business outlook does not seem to account entirely for the North Eastern's interest. H.A. Watson, General Superintendent of that railway, became a director of the Sand Hutton, and NER engineers surveyed the route and gave advice. Without their help, 'the little railway . . . could never have been started', wrote Sir Robert Walker, adding that it was 'quite impossible to pay an adequate tribute to the sympathy and kindness which . . . one and all showed'.[*]

The 15-inch gauge material was sold. *Synolda* rested in the tunnel until a purchaser was found, after which all certain knowledge of her was lost for many years – there were persistent rumours that she had gone to Ravenglass, even a paragraph in *The Railway Magazine*[†] supporting that theory, but there was never more than one Bassett-Lowke Atlantic in Eskdale, and *Sans Pareil* had been there since 1915. An enquiry addressed to the General Manager in December 1927, asking whether Sand Hutton material had been bought, drew only the dismissive reply that the information could not be supplied. However, there is little doubt that the Ravenglass & Eskdale Railway acquired the Bassett-Lowke four-wheelers, and no doubt whatever that they had the saloon coach which had been built in the Sand Hutton workshops, for this vehicle was well known to contemporary employees, and I myself saw and photographed it in the carriage shed at Ravenglass on 11 August 1924. Known there as The Glass Coach from its multiplicity of windows, it had one entrance on each side, at the left-hand end as one faced it, giving access to a small vestibule from which a sliding door led into the saloon. Within, reversible seats on each side of a gangway seated ten passengers. As

[*]   *The Railway Magazine*, vol. 55, p. 437.
[†]   Ibid., vol. 70, May 1932, p. 387.

its weight was no more than half a ton, it proved very useful when winter services in Eskdale were drawn by a light-weight internal combustion locomotive.

The contrast between the elegant 15-inch gauge stock and that obtained from the War Surplus Disposals Board in 1921 was stark, for the locomotives and wagons were strictly utilitarian, all with wooden dumb buffers, three-link couplings, four wheels and very short wheelbase to negotiate the curves within the meat depot, but they were sturdily built and in good condition. Seventy-five of the very simple wagons, built in 1915 by P. & W. Maclellan of Glasgow, were purchased; these were 7ft. long over the buffers and had a box-like body of 2in. plank with drop sides which could be removed, enabling two to be used as bogies to carry any long load such as tree trunks, timbers, girders, and even clover and hay on improvised floors 16ft. long. The side members of the frame were prolonged to form the buffers, and each of the end cross-members was strengthened by a steel plate to take the hook and coil spring of the coupling. Unbraked, and riding on unsprung axleboxes and disc wheels 18in. diameter, these little wagons had a wheelbase of 2ft. a tare weight of 1 ton 4 cwt. and a capacity of 2½ tons.

The locomotives, built by the Hunslet Engine Company of Leeds in 1915–17, were of a well-tried lightweight industrial design dating back to the 1890s. Three, Hunslet works numbers 1289, 1290 and 1291 of 1917, were obtained in 1921, and a fourth, number 1207 of 1916, was added in 1927. The builder's plates were of course retained, but surprisingly, throughout their Sand Hutton service the Deptford plates numbered 10, 11, 12 and 4 were also retained. They had outside frames, outside cylinders 6½in. diameter with 8in. stroke, coupled wheels 18½in. diameter, heating surface 96 sq. ft. (tubes 78, firebox 18), working pressure 160lb. per sq. in., and their weight in working order was 5 tons 19 cwt. Cylindrical sand boxes were mounted on the boiler fore and aft of the steam dome. Wheelbase was only 3ft. 6in., but the overhang in front, where the water tank was between the frames behind the buffer beam and under the smokebox, was 4ft. 3in., and at the rear end, where a large cab with open back was mounted on the footplate, it was 4ft. 9in. As Sir Robert commented, riding would have been much improved had there been a pair of leading or trailing wheels.

As supplied to Deptford, they had been fitted to burn oil fuel, but there was a change to coal firing later and their shapely little chimneys were disfigured by ugly spark-arresters – a kind of outsize casserole with a hole in the lid. Obviously these could not be tolerated at Sand Hutton, and they were replaced by neat copper caps. For winter working, the estate workshop provided wooden back-sheets with spectacles to enclose the cab when

Oil-burning 0–4–0 tank locomotive built in 1915 by the Hunslet Engine Co., Leeds (Works Number 1198), for the War Department Meat Depot at Deptford. The illustration, reproduced from the builder's leaflet, shows the smart finish with paintwork lined out and polished brass dome. This was not one of the engines sold to Sir Robert Walker, but went to a firm near Burton-on-Trent where it remained in use until 1958.

No. 12 at Warthill, 23 July 1927, George Batty driving.

The bogie coach for the 18-inch gauge line loaded on a North Eastern Railway dropside bogie wagon for delivery from Robert Hudson Ltd., Gildersome Foundry, Leeds in 1924. Photograph supplied by the builders.

necessary, and fitted a bracket in front of the chimney to take an acetylene car lamp. Livery was dark green. One, No. 10 named *Esmé* after the second Lady Walker, was fitted with the vacuum brake for working the passenger trains, but the unfitted No. 12 frequently took her place.

The tractive effort was 2,192lb. at 75 per cent of the boiler pressure, equal to hauling a load of 130 tons on the level* and 50 tons over the gradients north-east of Sand Hutton. One of the illustrations to Sir Robert's article in the May 1924 issue of *The Railway Magazine* shows a train at Warthill with no less than twenty-seven laden wagons and a van, totalling perhaps just over 100 tons, but he stated that the average load was 30 to 40 tons.

For the passenger service, two new vehicles were supplied by Robert Hudson Limited. One was a superior bogie coach 32ft. 9in. long overall and 4ft. 9in. wide; exceptional dimensions, indeed the builders believed it to be the largest ever built for such a narrow gauge. Delivered in 1924, it was fitted with spring buffers, three-link couplings, vacuum brake, torpedo

---

*   Hunslet's advertised load for locomotives of this type was 115 tons on the level. 130 tons was the figure given by Sir Robert Walker.

Four-wheeled brake van completed at the Gildersome Foundry in 1923. Photograph supplied by
Robert Hudson Ltd.

ventilators and electric light. Entry was from end platforms, and the interior
was divided into three sections: a long centre saloon with a lowered floor in a
well between the bogies; a saloon open to one of the end platforms and
having unglazed sides protected by waterproof curtains; and a private saloon
with moveable chairs and a table which enabled it to be used as a buffet. It
weighed 6 tons 5 cwt., and seated thirty on the slatted longitudinal seats in
two of the sections, and at least six in the private saloon. This sufficed for
most of the passenger carrying, but when special parties arranged a visit or
trains were run when a fête was held in the grounds, there was an overflow
into the brake van and sometimes even into cleaned up wagons! The livery
was burnt sienna, and it bore the initials SH in gold and brown lettering. As
built, the elliptical roof reached from end to end over the balconies, but this
created a hazard to passengers as they mounted from the step to the
platform, and it was no doubt as a result of cracked heads that neatly curved
incisions were soon introduced over each entrance.

The other vehicle, built in 1923, was a four-wheeled brake van to run with the coach on passenger trains, but it was also used on the heaviest of the freight trains to supplement the engine brakes on the 1 in 80 gradients. With a length of 15ft., it overhung its 6ft. wheelbase by a considerable amount at each end, one of which had a platform whereon the guard stood to operate the screw-down brake wheel. The wooden body had a sliding door on each side, and could carry up to 4 tons of parcels or other goods needing protection from the weather, yet its tare weight was only some 36 cwt. Like the wagons, it had dumb buffers and three-link couplings.

Five stations were provided: Warthill, Sand Hutton Central, Memorial (beside the Sand Hutton and Claxton War Memorial at a road junction), Kissthorns and Bossall. Although the Light Railway Order had stated that neither platforms nor shelters need be provided, all five stations had a low platform of gravel neatly edged by boarding, and Central and Bossall each had a shelter. In addition to the five stations, there were four halts.

As always, the railway had to be inspected on behalf of the Ministry of Transport before being allowed to carry passengers. Sir Robert Walker was well known in transport circles and presently became a Member of the recently formed Institute of Transport.[*] Perhaps it was because any recommendations that might have to be put to one of his knowledge and standing must come from someone of great experience and authority, perhaps it was no more than a courteous gesture, but, whatever the reason, the inspection of the little railway was made by the Ministry's Chief Inspecting Officer, Colonel J.W. Pringle, Royal Engineers.[†] Very probably North Eastern and LNER officers had previously examined the equipment and given advice, for Colonel Pringle was satisfied and, after receiving his report, the Ministry authorised use of the line by passenger trains, the first of which ran on 4 October 1924.

In 1924 and 1925, there was a Wednesday service, but during most of the line's short life, trains ran on Saturdays only, three in each direction, all giving good connections to and from York at Warthill, the earliest enabling passengers to reach the city at 10.55 a.m. for the market. Limited to a

---

[*] The Institute of Transport was founded in 1919 and incorporated by Royal Charter in 1926. Major Sir Robert Walker, Bt., was elected Member on 5 January 1925, and the present Librarian of the Chartered Institute tells me that the designation 'Member' was then the senior of the two professional grades, and that the equivalent today would be 'Fellow'.

[†] Colonel Pringle had had much railway experience as an officer of the Royal Engineers. He was a Member of the Institution of Civil Engineers, and Chief Inspecting Officer of Railways from 1916 until his retirement in 1929. In 1925, he was knighted as Sir John Pringle.

maximum speed of 12 mph, stopping so many times, and having to reduce speed to 4 mph at the level crossings, trains were allowed 40 minutes to cover the 5.2 miles, an average of just over 7¾ mph, though practice journeys were often completed in less time. Tickets of thin card, similar to contemporary tram and bus tickets, were issued on the trains by the conductor-guard, and the fare for the whole journey between Warthill and Bossall, probably unaltered over the years, was 8*d.* in 1927. Although the timetable stated that tea and light refreshments would be available on all except the early morning train, it is not clear how regularly this was done; perhaps it depended on the number and inclination of the passengers – I was certainly served on one of my visits.

Some visitors were drawn by the novelty of the railway, especially York schoolboys, but passenger traffic never amounted to much, no more than thirty to forty a week at the best of times. When there was a fête in the Hall grounds, however, a train ran merrily from Sand Hutton to White Sike Junction or Kissthorns, carrying passengers for sixpence a time, but as the takings were given to charities, especially the Welfare Association of the Coldstream Guards, Sir Robert's former regiment, it is unlikely that those numbers were ever included in the official returns.

Freight traffic, however, was considerable for the few years before motor lorries began to erode it. Outward from the farms, especially those served direct by a siding, went potatoes, hay and clover, sugar beet (about 300 tons in a good season), as well as more general produce. The entire production of the Claxton Brickworks, some 20,000 bricks a day, was carried by rail, as the bridle-way which ran past was quite unfit for lorries; some of the bricks travelled no more than a quarter of a mile to the Claxton terminus beside the York–Malton road, but the bulk of them went to Warthill for transhipment. Inward came fertilizers and cattle cake for the farms, flour and general merchandise and, above all, coal, 50 tons a week going to the brickworks alone. In fact, for a time, coal accounted for some 2,700 of the 13,000 tons of freight carried annually.

The railway I knew in 1927–8 was therefore very much alive. As with all narrow gauge lines, it had strong individuality and its own idiosyncrasies. The most marked was the method of replenishing the locomotive water tank which, with a limited capacity of 58 gallons, had to be refilled during every trip. Surprisingly, there was no storage tank with a water-crane, but wells had been sunk at Sand Hutton depot and the Bossall terminus, and there was a stream crossed by the railway at White Sike Cottages from which the Claxton branch engine could draw water – and it was indeed a matter of *drawing*, in a bucket, and pouring through a funnel, so the regular equipment

Bucket hanging from the handle of the smokebox door, funnel in the orifice of the water tank and the eager interest of the schoolboy! (*NGRS: Ken Hartley Collection.*)

Warthill transhipment sidings. The narrow gauge wagons on the high level were loaded with bricks for transfer; those on the left had received a consignment of coal. 2 July 1927.

of an engine included a bucket generally hanging from the handle of the smokebox door and a funnel standing below in the orifice of the tank!

The Warthill passenger station needed no shelter because it stood alongside the LNER station where, in inclement weather, passengers could wait until the narrow gauge train arrived. The goods yard, however, was well equipped for transhipment: on either side of a standard gauge siding was a narrow gauge track, one on the same level, the other rising by an embankment to reach a high level brick-built platform. All outward freight was therefore passed downward from narrow gauge to standard gauge, and inward traffic also was handed down from the higher wagon floor to the lower one. Labour-intensive though this was, Sir Robert Walker reckoned in 1924 that it was in the long run the cheapest and most efficient method. In 1927, however, he decided, as well he might, that there was a more economical way of handling bricks, and in the latter part of July, LNER engineers installed for him apparatus obtained from Herbert Morris of Loughborough. A steel gantry straddled the high-level siding and was able to travel from end to end on rails; it carried tackle capable of lifting one ton and of moving sideways in guides extending over the standard gauge siding. The bricks were loaded on trays at Claxton, and at Warthill these trays were raised and run out above the floor of the main-line wagon — but even so, every brick had to be shifted by hand from the trays.

The journey to Bossall passed through beautiful, even if small scale, scenery, much of it of course being part of a well cared for estate. Soon after leaving Warthill, the track ran alongside a private bridle-road, dead straight for a mile, and on one of my visits when there was no other passenger, George Batty let me drive along here until, inevitably, I allowed the speed to rise too high — apparently this was also a failing of Sir Robert's, but as he could not be as rapidly supplanted as I was, his driver had to await an opportunity to ease the regulator back unseen!

Then came White Sike Junction where the main line quitted the bridle-way, swinging to the right into a narrow clearing through a thick fir wood, the track bordered on both sides by a gorgeous riot of rhododendrons. On open ground beyond was Sand Hutton Depot with sidings and a two-road engine shed, well built of timber on a brick plinth and roofed by an almost semi-circular covering of corrugated iron topped by a ventilated clerestory; within, a bench, hand tools and drills enabled light repairs to be carried out.

After climbing at 1 in 80 up a low embankment, crossing a three-span bridge formed of old rails embedded in concrete piers, and passing into deciduous woodland, the line reached Sand Hutton Central, a very attractive spot surrounded by noble trees. Moreover, as the most important station on

Train at White Sike Junction, where the line to Sand Hutton turned off to the right and the Claxton branch continued alongside the bridle-road straight ahead through the wood. Photograph by Catcheside of York.

Sand Hutton Depot, George Batty standing beside No. 10 *Esmé*. 23 July 1927.

Sand Hutton Central station, 2 July 1927: neat gravel platform, glazed timber shelter, platform
seats and a contemporary car on the level crossing!

the railway, it was furnished with a glazed wooden shelter, platform seats,
and – think of it – slot machines which dispensed cigarettes for sixpence or a
penny! Beyond the level crossings of a public road and the private carriage
drive, there was another wood, which I described at the time as a birds'
paradise, before reaching Gardens Halt.

Leaving the wood and climbing again at 1 in 80, the line passed Memorial
station, and in open pastoral country ran close beside a bridle-road to
Kissthorns, the summit of the line, 74ft. above Warthill, and the loading
point for substantial traffic from neighbouring farms. There were extensive
views over the Wolds to the north before the descent towards the Derwent
valley began, passing through one of the few cuttings of any appreciable
depth and then curving sharply as it followed the field boundaries on the
way to the terminus at Bossall. As this station was a quarter of a mile from
the village, an open-fronted timber shelter was thoughtfully provided for
waiting passengers. Beyond the running round loop, a siding marked the
start of the intended route to Scrayingham, and a half-mile branch led
steeply up at 1 in 65 to Barnby House.

The Claxton branch carried no passenger traffic, but Sir Robert gave
permission for myself and a friend, also from the North Eastern Area

Claxton Brickworks receiving supplies of coal. 26 November 1927.

Claxton terminus, abutting on Whinny Lane. 19 February 1928.

Headquarters at York, to travel over it on the roomy footplate with George Batty. From White Sike Junction it kept to the bridle-way through the fir plantation as far as the level crossing of the main road to Sand Hutton village, whereafter it ran in the open almost at surface level, with easy gradients but very sharp curves as it edged around the fields. Passing the busy brickworks, the running line led on for a quarter of a mile beside another bridle-way to the freight terminus at Whinny Lane, the road to Claxton village and Bossall. One of the sidings entered the only goods shed on the railway, within which a loading bench enabled farm fertilizers and produce to be handled or stored under cover.

Traffic operation was extremely simple. There were no signals, so approach to the level crossings of the six more important roads was marked at a distance of 200 yards by a white board at the trackside bearing a triple V in black letters, and road users were warned to 'beware of trains' by a board placed about 50 yards away. Goods trains were not operated according to a timetable but were run as required, those carrying a full load running from starting point to Warthill at passenger train speeds, those calling at farm sidings of course taking much longer. For five or six years, there was enough work for two locomotives to be in steam daily, one of which kept to the Claxton branch, the other to the main line for that day. But how was use of the common line between the junction and Warthill controlled? Collision was very unlikely where visibility was good along a mile of straight track, but confrontation from which one train would have had to retreat would have been awkward.

Precautions were of course taken on Saturdays when the passenger train was running. All points to be traversed had then to be locked, and the driver carried a red disc which he hung on a white board at the junction, notifying the driver of a freight train arriving from Claxton that the line ahead was occupied and that he must stop and await the return of the passenger train from Warthill. Primitive though this method was, it worked satisfactorily, but it would certainly not have satisfied a Ministry of Transport Inspector! I described it in the draft of the article I wrote for the *Locomotive Railway Carriage & Wagon Review*, but after this had been submitted to Sir Robert Walker, all mention of the red disc had to be suppressed!

Accidents of any kind were, in fact, very few, and those that did occur were in no way due to operating methods. Ken Hartley, whose informative little book★ covers the later history of the railway, remarked that 'there is no

---

★ Hartley, K.E., *The Sand Hutton Light Railway*, Narrow Gauge Railway Society, 1964, revised edition 1982, p. 54.

record of anybody ever getting injured'. One engine, No. 12, presumably riding unsteadily, struck a tree stump beside the track with enough force to bend her buffer beam. Sometimes movement was so vigorous that engine and coach buffers locked, throwing the front bogie off the rails; indeed, this happened often enough for the train crew to carry a sturdy timber with which to re-rail the bogie. The engine of a goods train, which was derailed on a sharp curve on top of an embankment, came to rest propped against a tree, saving it from a serious fall and the driver from probable injury. There were, of course, some near misses: the cuttings through clay near Bossall were inadequately drained, so that after heavy rain sleepers were liable to sink and track to be distorted but, surprisingly, damage seems to have been confined to the driver's nerves. When rails were slippery, engine and van brakes were unable to control heavily-laden trains descending the 1 in 80 gradient from Kissthorns to Sand Hutton, making it impossible to reduce speed, let alone stop, at the level crossings, so that safe passage depended on agonised whistling and luck – but somehow the luck always held! One of the many York schoolboys privileged to enjoy a footplate ride once took advantage of the driver's momentary absence while picking up some goods, fiddled, opened the regulator, and lost his head when the engine moved; looking wildly round, he saw the driver gesticulating, fortunately read the signs correctly, and was able to shut off steam.

The railway was run economically. The Sand Hutton estate agent, S.C. Foster, was Secretary and Manager. George Batty, who had been estate engineer before Robert Walker inherited the property, was not only senior driver, but also attended to railway maintenance both civil and mechanical, saw to day-to-day organisation, and handled much office work. Other members of his family helped voluntarily, for when a buffet car attendant was needed, one of his daughters served the refreshments which had been provided by her mother. There was one other driver; a guard who manned the van and, when it was attached to the passenger coach, issued the tickets; and three or four goods porters who loaded and unloaded wagons, one of whom occasionally acted as relief driver – a total of six or seven.

Sir Robert believed strongly in the service a light railway could render to farming. Time would have enabled him to prove his belief, but in the early 1920s the time was not available. If four years of war had not interrupted his management of the estate and, more significantly, forced rapid development of the internal combustion engine, he would have extended his 15-inch gauge garden railway to serve the farms, using locomotives much larger and more powerful than *Synolda*, and at that date obtainable at reasonable prices. It would then have had many years in which to establish itself before having

No. 12 on the embankment between Sand Hutton Central and the depot, halted by George Batty for me to take the photograph before rejoining the train. The alteration made to the roof of the passenger coach is obvious. 2 July 1927.

to face the competition of motor lorries. The years 1920–3, however, were far too late for such a railway to have lasting success.

As it was, the maximum tonnage of freight carried was 13,650 in 1928, and the maximum number of passengers 2,185 in 1925. The average for the four years 1925–8 was 11,044 tons and 1,559 passengers, but in 1929–30 this fell to 4,843 tons and 428 persons – in fact, in 1930 only 65 people travelled. Although the net receipts for 1924–9 showed an accumulated profit of £421, this was less than a quarter of the interest that had been paid on the debentures. Thereafter, gross receipts did not cover working expenses.

Sir Robert Walker died on 11 February 1930, a month short of his fortieth birthday. The Claxton Brickworks closed in 1931, having exhausted the local deposit of clay. Although some farmers on the estate still relied on the railway, others had turned to road transport to avoid three transhipments of their produce. As all were suffering from the general depression in agriculture and industry, the Trustees saw no likelihood of the railway ever recovering enough traffic to justify keeping it open. The last passenger train ran on 7 July 1930 and, after the Ministry of Transport had consented to closure, all traffic ceased in June 1932, and the company was wound up on

24 October. The scrap merchants, T.W. Ward of Sheffield, took rails, locomotives and rolling stock for disposal – all except the passenger coach which became a cricket pavilion.

Ken Hartley knew the railway, as I did, while it was still working, but he twice revisited the site long after it had closed and gathered information from those who still remembered it. He recorded that the locomotive shed housed poultry for a time, but either collapsed or was demolished in 1965. As no further members of the Walker family resided at the Hall, the beautiful grounds were neglected, until some time after 1960 when what remained of the house was pulled down and a select housing estate covered the park. By then little remained to show that there had ever been a railway of either gauge.

I am glad I never saw all this, so that my memories are of four happy afternoons in 1927–8 spent on an unusually intriguing little railway in a lovely setting of open fields, woods and rhododendron bushes, rich with the colours and scents of summer and the song of wild birds.

CHAPTER SIX

THE RESERVOIR CONSTRUCTION RAILWAY, COLSTERDALE

W hile I was a trainee in the service of the LNER,★ I was posted to Ripon Goods station from March to September 1928. The city has great charm, with a spacious market-place and an intriguing Minster which had become a cathedral in 1836, both situated on a hill from which the main road descends to cross the River Ure by the ancient North Bridge. Pastoral and arable land lies on either side of the river, but to the west and north-west is high moorland penetrated by dales of great beauty, the Ure itself flowing from Wensleydale.

There were pleasant summer evening walks by the river bank and along lanes and field paths near the city, and weekend bicycle rides in the Vale of York or into the dales, sometimes extended further afield by travelling on a branch-line train. One such branch served the market town of Masham, ten miles to the north-west of Ripon, where the River Burn from Colsterdale joins the Ure. This had been opened by the North Eastern Railway in 1875 from Melmerby on the main line of the former Leeds Northern Railway from Leeds through Harrogate and Ripon to Northallerton.

A quarter of a century before my sojourn in Ripon, both Harrogate and Leeds had chosen Colsterdale as a site for reservoirs, and in 1901 their plans

★ See *With the LNER in the Twenties*, Alan Sutton, 1985.

0–4–2 saddle tank locomotive *Harrogate* built by T. Green & Son, Leeds, for use by Harrogate Corporation in building Roundhill Reservoir. (*Collection: R.N. Redman.*)

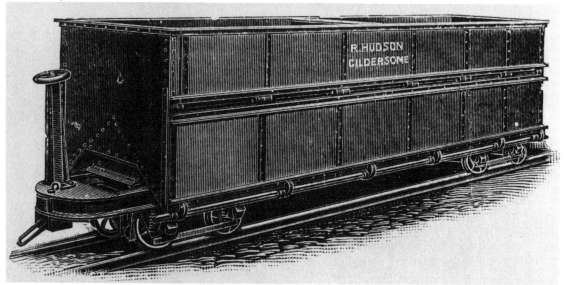

Bogie hopper wagon with side discharge supplied by Robert Hudson Ltd., Leeds. Illustration from the builder's catalogue sheet.

Harrogate with a party of visitors in one of the bogie cars with longitudinal back-to-back seats and footrails built by Robert Hudson Ltd. to carry workmen. The ladies appear rather overdressed for such an excursion! (*Collection R.N. Redman.*)

had been approved by Parliament. Soon afterwards, Harrogate Corporation began to build Roundhill Reservoir, not in the upper reach of Colsterdale from which flows the River Burn, but in the valley of its tributary, the Agill Beck, a little to the south where the geological conditions were more satisfactory.

Materials for the construction of dam, reservoir and conduit were carried by standard gauge trains to the goods yard at Masham terminus, but transport over the 6¼ miles beyond was less easy in a remote dale served by inferior country roads. Initially, the corporation engaged a haulage contractor to carry materials from Masham to a depot at Leighton, where the Agill Beck joins the Burn, but beyond Leighton there was no suitable road, so a 2ft. gauge railway was constructed from the depot to the site of the dam, about 1¾ miles beyond. The haulage contractor used steam traction engines with steel tyres grooved to provide a grip on the road surface, drawing large, steel-tyred, heavily-laden wagons, and very soon there were local complaints of the damage done, and substantial claims for the cost of repair

Trestle bridge across the Ure at Masham, the river flowing swiftly in the summer of 1928.

lodged by the highway authority. The corporation therefore decided to extend the railway from Leighton to Masham, and in 1904 obtained power to do so by the Harrogate Waterworks Tramroad Act. The following year it concluded an agreement with the North Eastern Railway for one of the sidings in Masham goods yard to be extended across a road into a field, where narrow gauge sidings were laid alongside and a gantry erected for transhipment of heavy material.

Harrogate had already acquired two steam locomotives, both built by T. Green & Son of Leeds, the first in 1902, an 0–4–2 saddle tank with cylinders 6in. × 10in., named *Harrogate*, and the second the following year, an 0–4–0 saddle tank with 7in. × 12in. cylinders, named *Claro*, the ancient Danish name of the area in which the town stood. The 4½-mile extension to Masham made a third engine necessary, and so an 0–6–2 saddle tank with 9½in. × 14in. cylinders was built by T. Green & Son in 1904 and named *Masham*.

Rolling stock was obtained from Robert Hudson Limited of Leeds, who in 1928 kindly supplied me with information and illustrations.★ There were

'Hydroleum' locomotive *Progress* built by Arn Jung and marketed by A. Koppel, supplied to Harrogate Corporation for use in driving the tunnel for the aqueduct from Roundhill Reservoir to the town. The design was based on that of a steam launch engine, oil fired. (*Collection R.N. Redman.*)

side-discharge bogie hopper wagons, about 20ft. long, 5ft. wide and 6ft. high, with a tare weight of 4¼ tons and a capacity of 350 cu. ft. and several peculiar passenger cars for workmen, roofed but with open sides and longitudinal back-to-back seats with footrails. Locally I was told that there had been an enclosed bogie saloon to carry visitors, but Hudsons had no record of having built any such vehicle, and only the workmen's cars appear in photographs.

Harrogate Corporation built the dam, reservoir and railway by direct labour, and its engineers had to cross some half-dozen roads on the level and erect five bridges over hill streams and the Rivers Ure and Burn, the two latter being considerable timber structures. The Ure was crossed soon after leaving Masham yard, where the river was wide and ran swiftly, especially when in spate, and the four-span bridge had therefore to be strongly built with massive timbers supported by three trestles rising from the water. That

★ Letter dated 5 April 1928.

across the Burn, approaching Leighton depot, was less substantial, the track being laid on the top of horizontal timbers resting on trestles and strengthened by diagonal members.

The construction camp was below the site of the dam, and it was to provide transport for the navvies to and from Masham on Saturdays that the passenger cars were needed; as the train seems to have been known locally as 'The Paddy Mail', it seems probable that a sizeable proportion of the work force was Irish. Stone for the dam was brought down to the spot by an incline from a quarry on the Arnagill Crags (or Clints Crags) to the east, and from a point below the dam a tunnel for the aqueduct was driven under the crags and Masham Moor, its south-easterly direction marked on the present-day Ordnance Survey maps by the position of the engineers' Sighting Towers. The 2ft. gauge railway extended into the tunnel and, for haulage within, two steam locomotives of special design were obtained – the first decade of the twentieth century was yet too early for petrol tractors. *May* was supplied by the German builder Koppel as an 0–4–0 with small side tanks, an upright water-tube boiler, oil-fired, which supplied steam at 250lb. pressure to a high-speed, four-cylinder vertical engine. Of the second engine, named *Progress*, no details are known, but she was probably of similar type from the same stable. Conditions in the tunnel must have been extremely unpleasant, for although spared smuts and cinders, enginemen and navvies alike were exposed to obnoxious oil fumes.

Before Roundhill Dam was completed in 1910, Leeds Corporation had begun preliminary work for construction of its reservoir, which it originally intended to form in upper Colsterdale where it would have been filled by the River Burn, but this site was abandoned when it was found that the geological conditions essential for water retention were not good enough. The railway, however, had already been extended in that direction from a junction at Leighton, and in January 1905 a locomotive had been obtained for working the corporation's trains over the line to Masham. Having to find another site for the reservoir, the engineers decided to place it immediately below Roundhill Dam, taking the water from the spillway and from the Grimes Gill untapped by Harrogate. In 1908 a contract for construction of an earth-filled dam, much longer and wider than Harrogate's, and for the reservoir (named Leighton after the nearby hamlet) was let to Arnold & Sons of Leeds and Doncaster. When Harrogate's need of the railway line to Masham had ceased, the town sold it to Leeds, and two of the engines, as well as the rolling stock, passed into the possession of the city corporation or its contractors.

Space for the Leeds construction camp could be found only at Breary

0–6–2 side tank locomotive *Leeds No. 1*, built by the Hunslet Engine Co. in 1904 for use by Leeds Corporation in building Leighton Reservoir. (*Collection R.N. Redman.*)

Bank beside the River Burn, close to the terminus of the railway already built, and to reach the site of the dam, which was considerably below that at Roundhill, trains had to reverse. Several other branch lines diverged from near the terminus: one to the camp, another down an incline to a power station, and a third to a source of outcrop stone. There were also various lines laid by the contractors to a gauge of 3ft., no doubt having equipment which they had used on previous contracts and deciding that the low wages then paid to unskilled labour made the cost of transhipment a better economic proposition than investing in 2ft. gauge track, engines and wagons! One of their lines was laid to the Clints Quarry excavated by Harrogate, but descended by a new incline on a different alignment in order to reach the site of Leighton dam.

Arnold & Sons used a dozen or more 3ft. gauge locomotives built by several different firms: Peckett of Bristol, W.G. Bagnall of Stafford, Hudswell Clarke & Co. of Leeds. They also took over *Claro* from Harrogate Corporation and acquired another 2ft. gauge engine, an 0–4–0 well tank named *Sidney* which had been built in Germany, probably by Koppel.

Rolling stock in Masham Yard in the summer of 1928, after completion of the reservoirs. Between the two narrow gauge tracks is the standard gauge siding extended from the North Eastern Railway goods yard.

The locomotive the city corporation had obtained in 1905 to work the Masham line was an 0–6–2 side tank built by the Hunslet Engine Company, Leeds (Works Number 865 of 1904), with cylinders 10¾in. × 15in., coupled wheels 2ft. 4in., trailing wheels 18in, heating surface 381 sq. ft. (tubes 345, firebox 36), pressure 160lb. per sq. in., weight in working order 18½ tons, tractive effort 7,425lb., capable of hauling 390 tons on the level, 195 tons up a gradient of 1 in 100 and 110 tons up 1 in 50. Hunslet's works photograph shows a plain unlined finish, but views of her in service show smart lining out and the legend *Leeds No. 1* on her tank side. Even so, however, the corporation took over the 0–6–2 tank engine *Masham* when Harrogate's need of it ceased, and used it for several years until 1912.

After the outbreak of war in August 1914, dam building slowed down as members of the work-force joined the colours, and in the autumn the army commandeered Breary Bank camp, enlarged it, and billeted troops there. Then early in 1915, all construction ceased, Arnold & Sons removed their 3ft. gauge material, and the following year Breary Bank became a prisoner-of-war camp. Meantime, the railway to Masham was kept busy carrying supplies and personnel – troops and guards could escape by train in search of entertainment in the pubs of Masham, but prisoners of war confined to the camp must have been acutely aware of its isolation.

Not until 1919 was work on the dam renewed, Leeds Corporation thenceforward employing direct labour and installing 2ft. gauge tracks on Arnold's abandoned formations. For additional motive power it acquired, no doubt from the War Surplus Disposals Board, Simplex petrol tractors, at least one of the 20 h.p. open type and one of the more powerful and heavier 40 h.p. variety which the Motor Rail & Tramcar Company had supplied to the War Department with two different forms of enclosed body, one 'protected', the other 'armoured'.

When dam and reservoir had been completed, the railway equipment was sold, some of it in July 1926. When I first visited Masham late in March 1928, various wagons were still in the narrow gauge yard awaiting disposal, and so was *Leeds No. 1*, carefully sheeted over and therefore impossible to photograph, but by the time of my second visit, during the early summer, she had gone. Two Simplex tractors remained, the 40 h.p. one temporarily out of service; its engine was lifted from the chassis and transferred to a bogie which was propelled by the 20 h.p. tractor up an improvised ramp to the back of a lorry, so that it could be sent away for repair. Evidently both were still needed to haul the odd assortment of wagons which stood in the yard, ready to carry rails and sleepers as the line was dismantled.

CHAPTER SEVEN

THE HARROGATE GAS COMPANY'S RAILWAY

W hile I was at Ripon, I had to make a number of journeys which took me through Bilton Junction, about 1½ miles north-east of the centre of Harrogate, where I was intrigued by the sight of a small narrow gauge tank locomotive which hauled wagons from transhipment sidings to the Harrogate Gas Works. When I was moved from Ripon to Harrogate Goods station in September 1928, I found 'digs' in Bilton where I was well placed to visit this little railway, 1¾ miles long. Its route was not direct as, in order to avoid cutting through high ground, it ran west and then south to reach the works alongside the Leeds–Ripon road. Even so, there had to be several stretches of stiff climbing at 1 in 20½–24 and an awkward tunnel 660 yards long.

The gasworks had been established in 1846 on the outskirts of the town, far from the main-line railway, and the coal had to be carried by horse and cart from Starbeck station nearly 3 miles away. Increased demand for gas made it essential to take delivery from somewhere nearer, and so in 1880 the Gas Company and the North Eastern Railway installed the sidings at Bilton Junction, whence traction engines hauled trains of four 7-ton road wagons. Inevitably, this traffic severely damaged the road surface, and the Gas Company was saddled with the expense of maintaining it.

After twenty years and the expenditure of £6,500, a less costly method had to be found. Harrogate Corporation, mindful of its own need of coal for an electricity generating station, joined with the Gas Company in an appeal to the North Eastern to share in the cost of building a standard gauge branch

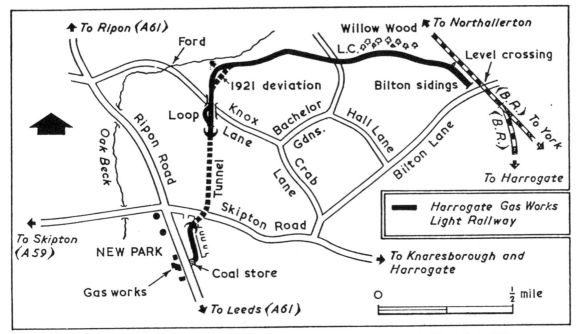

Map of the Harrogate Gas Company's Railway. ('*The Railway Magazine*', vol. 115, 1969, p. 435.)

line, but the railway, taking the not unreasonable view that this was not their concern, showed little inclination to help. The corporation therefore suggested that the Gas Company should build a narrow gauge railway as it had done for the waterworks in Colsterdale, so in 1904 the directors visited Masham, and afterwards decided that this would indeed be the best course to adopt.

To survey a route from Bilton to the works, the company engaged the same engineer who had been employed in Colsterdale and, armed with his report, invited tenders for the construction of a 2ft. gauge line capable of carrying 10,000 tons a year. Then, calling its shareholders to a special meeting, the company asked for approval of the project and for authority to increase its capital to meet the estimated cost of £20,000. The shareholders having given their consent, work began on 25 April 1907.

The contractors were a Liverpool firm, and they began by sinking a shaft 53½ ft. deep on the line of the tunnel, completion of which was certain to take longer than the rest of the railway. As the head of the shaft was no place for a celebration, the ceremony of cutting the first sod was held on 7 May at a spot in an open field readily accessible by road. It was attended by the Mayor and Town Clerk of Harrogate, the Vicar of Bilton, the engineer E.W. Dixon, and the Gas Company's Chairman, F. Barber. The traditional silver spade was provided, the vicar read prayers, a partner in the contracting firm made a speech and there was of course a luncheon.

0–6–2 saddle tank locomotive *Barber* built by T. Green & Son, Leeds, 1908. Autumn 1928.

Twinberrow all-steel bogie hopper wagon, 10 ton capacity, built 1908. At Bilton Junction transhipment sidings, February 1929.

Coal drops at Bilton. Narrow gauge wagons stand below the storage hoppers filled from the
North Eastern wagons, which varied in capacity from 10½ to 20 tons, the latter with tall tapering
sides. In the foreground is the curious wooden-bodied vehicle built by the Gas Company with a
bogie at one end and a single fixed axle at the other. Autumn 1928.

From tank wagons on the high-level narrow gauge siding at Bilton Junction, tar is being
discharged by gravity into standard gauge tar tank wagons. Autumn 1928.

Meantime, a locomotive had been ordered from Peckett & Sons of Bristol, the well-known builders of small industrial steam engines for various gauges, but as a dispute arose as to who should be liable for the cost of carriage to the gasworks, the order was cancelled and placed instead with T. Green & Son, whose works at Leeds were so much nearer and who, moreover, had supplied Harrogate Corporation with the three locomotives used on the waterworks railway. The engine was delivered early in 1908 and set to work hauling construction trains until haulage of coal over part of the line became possible in July, and over the whole of it in November.

The overall dimensions of the locomotive (builder's number 441) were severely limited by those of the tunnel, which was made only 9ft. high and 8ft. wide, so her chimney was short and her cab roof low. Even then, however, there was so little clearance between the engine and the lining of the tunnel that the back of the footplate had to be fitted with a small door through which the driver would be able to escape if the locomotive should fail while inside. Named *Barber* after the chairman, she was an 0–6–2 saddle tank with driving wheels 2ft. 6in. diameter, trailing wheels 18in., outside cylinders 10in. diameter with a stroke of 16in. and a boiler with 350 sq. ft. heating surface and a working pressure of 155lb. per sq. in., giving her a tractive effort of 7,000lb. Her weight was 19 tons empty. The livery was light green above red underframes.

Six large Sheffield-Twinberrow all-steel bogie wagons with twin hoppers were obtained, each 26ft. long, weighing 4 tons and having a capacity for 10 tons of coal, and two bogie wagons with cylindrical tanks to carry 5 tons of the valuable by-products of tar and other liquids from the gasworks for transhipment to the NER at Bilton. There was also a wooden-bodied hopper wagon which had been built by the Gas Company with a most unusual wheel arrangement, a two-axle bogie at one end and a single fixed axle at the other; it was used during construction of the line, and remained for many years carrying locomotive coal.

At Bilton Junction, the narrow gauge tracks were well below those of the standard gauge so that coal could be dropped from North Eastern bottom-door wagons into four storage hoppers from which the Gas Company's wagons were fed as required. One narrow gauge siding extended beyond the yard and climbed steeply to reach a platform alongside, but at a higher level than, the North Eastern siding, so that liquids could be discharged by gravity from one set of tank wagons to the other. It was on this platform that I had first seen the engine.

The track was substantial, formed with flat-bottomed rails weighing 40lb. per yard spiked to timber cross-sleepers in the open and to longitudinal

The northern portal of the tunnel, 9ft. high and 8ft. wide.

baulks through the tunnel. As the line was unfenced, cattle-guards had to be provided at the intersections of field boundaries to stop beasts straying. At first these were formed with the familiar wooden beams of triangular section placed with a sharp edge uppermost; later these were replaced by barriers, each of which had to be opened for the passage of a train and closed behind it, causing intolerable delay, so before long those were also replaced. The final solution was to dig a pit, line it with concrete and carry each rail across on a girder too narrow for the hooves of cattle.

Part of the tunnel was driven through rock, part built by the cut-and-cover method, and it was lined throughout with concrete 12in. or 15in. thick, reinforced by a 14in. brick arch where it passed under the A59 York–Skipton road. It is usual to construct a tunnel (except one passing under water) either on a slope throughout to one end, or from some intermediate point to each end, so that it will drain naturally, but it was not possible to adopt either course in the Gas Company's tunnel. Only 130 yards from the southern exit it had to pass below the Skipton road, and to reach

4–6–0 side tank locomotive, one of the first batch of ten built by the Hunslet Enging Co., Leeds, in 1916 for the War Department. Illustration from the builder's catalogue sheet.

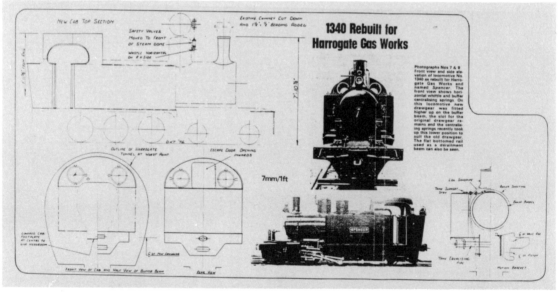

Hunslet Works Number 1340, completed in February 1919, was rebuilt by Hunslet in 1920 to fit the restricted dimensions of the tunnel. The Gas Company named her *Spencer*. (*Courtesy: Hunslet Engine Co.*)

the works yard about 350 yards beyond involved an awkward S-bend and an ascent at 1 in 54½ in the tunnel and 1 in 22½ beyond. Had there been a descent from the low point beneath the road to the northern entrance, the tunnel would have been very much longer and more expensive to build. Water therefore drained from both ends to a sump at the lowest point where the tunnel passed under the main road, but how this was drawn off is not apparent; there is no mention of pumping, so an adit seems probable.

The nicely-designed north portal was built of concrete, but by 1928 its appearance had been spoilt by those stains which always mar the surface of that material after a time; and of course there was the inevitable black streak from the exhaust of a hard-working locomotive.

In the early days, trains of two laden hopper wagons and two tank wagons returning empty were run from Bilton only two or three times a week, but as the use of gas spread, the tonnage of coal increased beyond the haulage capacity of a single engine, so when engines built to order of the War Department for service on the 60cm. gauge light railways of the Western Front became available from the War Surplus Disposals Board, the Gas Company bought one of the Hunslet Engine Company's reliable 4–6–0 side tank engines (Works Number 1340). As she had been completed in February 1919, she had never seen war service but, although brand new, she had to be returned to the Hunslet works for extensive modification to enable her to run on 2ft. gauge track and pass through the constricted tunnel. The very slight increase in gauge was readily achieved by moving the tyres and repositioning the brake gear. The height of the chimney was reduced and the safety valves moved from the top of the dome to its front, but a new and lower cab roof had to be built, the middle part of the footplate sunk between the frames to make room for the driver's feet, and the back sheet provided with a very small door so that the driver could get out by climbing over the bunker in case of need. New draw gear was fitted and the position of the centre buffer-coupling raised. Thus modified, she was painted black, named *Spencer* after the Gas Company's vice-chairman, and delivered to Harrogate early in 1920. Her coupled wheels were 2ft. diameter, bogie wheels 18½in., cylinders 9½in. × 12in., heating surface 205 sq. ft. (tubes 168, firebox 37), working pressure 160lb. per sq. in. and weight in working order 14 tons 1 cwt. Her tractive effort of 5,415lb. was equal to hauling 286 tons on the level and 80 tons up a gradient of 1 in 50. *Spencer*'s arrival enabled *Barber* to be sent off to Hunslet in 1921 for a thorough overhaul, which included a new copper firebox and brass boiler tubes.

With 22 per cent less power than *Barber*, *Spencer* proved unable to manage the 1 in 21½ on the sharp curve where the railway turned from west to

0–6–0 saddle tank locomotive built by Peckett & Sons, Bristol, in 1944 for Harrogate. To the right of her can be seen the front end of the 0–6–0 diesel locomotive built by the Drewry Car Co. in 1949. (*Frank Jones.*)

south, so both gradient and curve were eased. At the same time, a passing loop was inserted nearby. But although the Hunslet 4–6–0s had earned a very good reputation in war service, *Spencer*'s performance was never quite what the Gas Company expected; probably they asked too much of her, for there were complaints that she did not steam freely and that her firebox and grate quickly became choked with clinker, which suggests that she was frequently overloaded and 'flogged'.

In 1943, it was decided to replace her, and a new locomotive was ordered from Peckett & Sons. Delivered in February 1944, this was an 0–6–0 saddle tank engine, very restricted in height like the others, painted black as *Spencer* had been, but unnamed though carrying on her tank sides her owner's title in full. The coupled wheels were 2ft. 3½in. diameter, cylinders 9½in. × 14in., and boiler pressure 200lb. per sq. in., considerably higher than that of either of the others and giving her a tractive effort of 7,810lb. All the same, it would have been wiser to specify carrying wheels to guide her round the curves, which would have avoided her tendency to spread the metals and suffer derailment until steel ties were inserted to maintain the gauge. *Spencer* was then withdrawn and in 1946 sold for scrap.

After forty year's service, *Barber* also had to be replaced. Her successor, delivered in 1949, was an 0–6–0 diesel built by the Drewry Car Company with a Gardner engine driving through a 4-speed gear box, fluid flywheel and a jack-shaft coupled to the wheels. Although weighing only 12 tons, this locomotive had a maximum tractive effort of 8,300lb. *Barber* was then acquired by the Narrow Gauge Railway Society and given to Leeds City Museum.

In the meantime, the original hopper wagons and tank wagons had been replaced – they had been hard worked, for the expected traffic of 10,000 tons a year had long since been exceeded, more than five times that amount passing in 1940. The new vehicles, including tank wagons with rectangular instead of cylindrical tanks, were supplied by Robert Hudson Limited. By 1953, the capacity of the railway was so far overtaxed that some coal was being brought in by road, and as experience showed that lorry transport was more economical (the Gas Company not having to maintain the roads!), the railway was abandoned to demolition contractors in November 1956. The Drewry diesel was sold and eventually found a home in Rhodesia, and the Peckett was bought by the Festiniog Railway, in whose hands it awaits restoration at Boston Lodge Works.

CHAPTER EIGHT

THE LYNTON & BARNSTAPLE RAILWAY

Halloo! Halloo! we'll follow it through
From Bratton to Porlock Bay!

★   ★   ★

Nightacott, Narracott, Hunnacott's passed,
Right for the North they race:
He's leading them straight for Blackmoor Gate,
And he's setting a pounding pace!

A Song of Exmoor
by Sir Henry Newbolt ★

Although the Lynton & Barnstaple Railway never went anywhere near Porlock Bay, nor could it be described as 'leading . . . straight', it did head north from Bratton Fleming to Blackmoor and on the way passed the three farms whose lovely names Newbolt introduced into his poem. There were also other 'cotts' near the track: Southacott (or Southcott) and Sprecott for example, the suffix 'cott' denoting an isolated cottage or a mean shelter for cattle or sheep such as were found in former days scattered over the wilds of Exmoor, and around some of which hamlets coalesced in course of time.

★   Quoted by the kind permission of Peter Newbolt, Sir Henry's grandson.

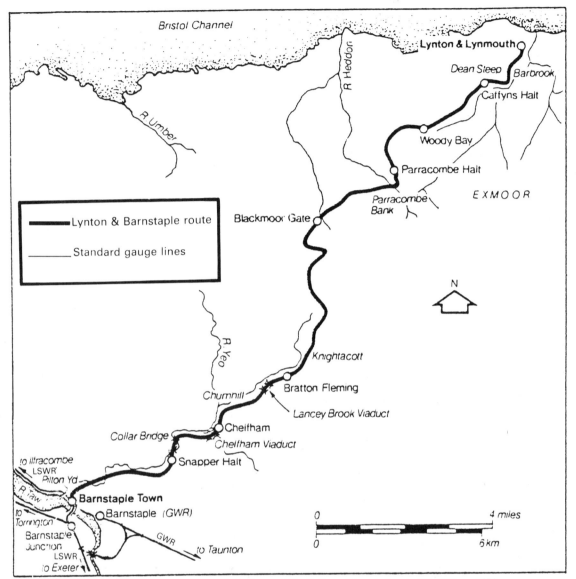

Map of the Lynton & Barnstaple Railway. ('*The Railway Magazine*', vol. 127, 1981, p. 137.)

And if the little locomotives never had the opportunity to 'race', they could at least be said to have set 'a pounding pace' as they breasted the steep gradients.

Probably, I first became aware of the existence of the railway from one of the Locomotive Publishing Company's coloured postcards which I collected avidly as a small boy whenever the pennies of pocket money permitted; they cost, if I remember aright, one penny each! Certainly I was on the look-out for the narrow gauge railway in 1915 as we travelled from Cheltenham Malvern Road station to Mortehoe for a family holiday at Woolacombe, North Devon. The Great Western had booked us via their Devon & Somerset branch from Taunton to Barnstaple, a tedious run with stops at eleven intermediate stations. Approaching Barnstaple I was on the alert, not realising that we still had to reverse in the GWR terminus and call at the Junction station before at last reaching Barnstaple Town, where I saw the Lynton train standing alongside in the bay platform.

Of course I clamoured for a ride on it; neither my mother nor my elder brother was interested, but my father (he was a wonderful father) at last succumbed to my importunity, so one day we toiled up the steep road for more than a mile and a half to Mortehoe station to catch the train to Barnstaple Town, and I was thrilled to have my first ride on a narrow gauge railway. We alighted at Woody Bay, where my father photographed the train for me. The railway was then only seventeen years old, and the second vehicle behind *Yeo* still had the white upper panels of the original livery.

It was a dozen years before I again travelled on the Lynton & Barnstaple, by which time it had been part of the Southern Railway for four years. Then, in August 1927, I made several journeys over the full length of the line and, provided with a letter from the Publicity Office at Waterloo, I was able to walk the track where I liked and, with the help of the friendly staff in Pilton Yard, to photograph the locomotives, including the American *Lynn* which was drawn out of the shed specially for me.

Two years earlier, the Southern had embarked on an extensive programme of improvement and renewal which the old company had been unable to afford. The original 40lb. per yard rails had been relaid and bedded in fresh ballast, the rails resting on sole-plates and secured to new sleepers by clips and bolts instead of the dog-spikes first used. Some curves had been eased, notably at Barbrook on the descent to Lynton. A new locomotive was obtained in 1925, and eight new goods vehicles in 1927. Coaches were overhauled, some fitted with steam heating for winter services and many with more comfortable seating for Third Class passengers. New signals and signal posts of LSWR pattern had replaced old ones, and fencing had been renewed to prevent cattle straying on the track and delaying trains. Accommodation at Lynton station was enlarged, improvements made at other stations and a staff canteen provided at Pilton.

No one could justly accuse the Southern of failing to do its best to ensure the success of the little railway, but by the late twenties and early thirties success was beyond reach, as many of the stations were inconveniently placed and local people found it easier to use the road services. In the latter

Recently relaid track on an embankment near Bratton Fleming station: fresh ballast, rails secured by clips bolted to new sleepers. 11 August 1927.

part of the nineteenth century, it had been very different. Exmoor then was a remote and wild area, beautiful but backward and sparsely populated, its inhabitants earning a precarious living by growing rye and oats on the scanty soil, from flocks of moorland sheep and sea fishing. Yet there were small settlements on or near the coast, such as Ilfracombe, Combe Martin, Lynton, Lynmouth and Minehead which could be reached by sea and were becoming known as quiet and attractive resorts, capable of expansion. As the railway network spread far and wide over Britain, inevitably there were suggestions that such places ought to be made accessible by rail, suggestions that came for the most part from entrepreneurs rather than local inhabitants or landowners, the latter resenting any interference with their freedom to hunt and shoot over a wide expanse of country and fish the rivers and hill streams in solitude.

Barnstaple, the most important town in North Devon, was reached in 1854 by the North Devon Railway, later part of the London & South Western Railway line from Exeter, and in 1873 by the Devon & Somerset, soon after absorbed by the GWR. In 1874, Minehead was reached from

Taunton, and Ilfracombe from Barnstaple. From these railheads, coach services began to run to Lynton, one or more a day in summer, one a week in winter, drawn by four horses which had to be assisted by one or even two more up the formidable hills at Countisbury and Porlock on the edge of Exmoor. Barnstaple, Ilfracombe and Minehead are each 16 miles from Lynton, and the coach journey took about three hours. A railway was the only way of providing quicker access; but a railway penetrating Exmoor? Neither of the two great companies was prepared to build a branch line which would be expensive to construct and unlikely to cover working expenses, let alone earn a return on the capital invested, and although several schemes were promoted independently, they received very limited support. A narrow gauge railway or a standard gauge electric tramway, either of which could be built more cheaply, appeared to be the only solution, and a Bill for a tramway might have been passed had not Parliament been dissolved in 1892.

However, a proposal that a line resembling the successful Festiniog Railway should be built to the same narrow gauge of 1ft. 11½in. gained powerful support from Sir George Newnes, a Member of Parliament and well known as the publisher of widely read magazines which included *Country Life, The Strand Magazine* and *Tit-Bits*. He was joined by his friend, Thomas Hewitt KC, with whom he had stayed before deciding to make Lynton his holiday home, and by E.B. Jeune of Lynton Manor and W.H. Halliday, another influential local personality. Following their lead, local support was forthcoming, but selection of the best route was hampered by the opposition of some landowners whose property had therefore to be avoided, and by the insistence of the promoters that the railway should not spoil the scenic beauties. Nevertheless, the capital of £72,000 was quickly subscribed and the Bill incorporating the company was enacted on 27 June 1895. No time was lost in making a start, and on 17 September Lady Newnes cut the first sod.

Sir James Szlumper, a railway engineer of note (other Szlumpers were closely involved in the affairs of the LSWR and the Southern), was appointed Consulting Engineer, and the tender of J. Nuttall of Manchester to build the line for £42,100 was accepted. So far, so good, but troubles soon beset the enterprise. Some landowners who were in favour of the railway nevertheless demanded such high prices for the strip needed for the right of way that the total cost of land turned out to be three times that allowed for in the estimates. The geological conditions had not been sufficiently examined because it had been assumed that, in the main, the line would follow the surface and there would be a minimum of earth shifting, but it seems not to

Rock cutting near Bratton Fleming. *Lew* piloting *Exe* on a train of a van and five coaches.
11 August 1927.

have been realised that following the contours involved cutting a ledge along the hillside and that this would quickly penetrate the scanty topsoil to the rock below, that cuttings through rock would have to be blasted, and that not all the little combs could be circumvented but would have to be crossed by embankments and bridges. The cost of construction had therefore been grossly underestimated and the contractor misled when preparing his tender; in fact, the cost exceeded by more than 40 per cent the £50,000 calculated.

The more difficult conditions encountered delayed completion of the railway by a year, and led to the contractor submitting a claim for £40,000 extra which, under the terms of the contract, the company had every right to dispute; but Szlumper as arbitrator awarded Nuttall a further £27,000 and although the company resorted to litigation and won the case, Nuttall was bankrupted and the company was unable to recover costs. Moreover, it had to complete the works itself. All this could have been avoided had Szlumper examined the ground with proper care and made a more realistic estimate of the cost, enabling the company to raise more capital in the first place and saving it from the embarrassment of overstrained financial resources.

Other mistakes were made, notably in the site chosen for the Lynton terminus, 250ft. above the town when it might have been placed lower and nearer but for the opposition of a landowner whom the company could not afford to compensate. Furthermore, the station never had a supply of water adequate to the needs of a terminus because the Lynton Water Company proposed to levy a heavy rate for delivery at that height; what little was available from a hill stream soon failed in a dry summer, and then even use of the station lavatories had to be banned!

On the other hand, the railway was equipped with track, station buildings and signalling of a high standard, perhaps higher than necessary for the Light Railways Act was passed on 14 August 1896 before the railway had been completed, so that some advantage might have been taken of its provisions. As it was, more money had to be raised even before the line could be opened, and more still in 1905, some of it by issuing new shares, some in the form of debentures and loans, with the result that the shareholding had risen to £84,976 and the debt to £42,200 by the date of absorption by the Southern Railway.

The railway was ready for examination by the Board of Trade Inspector, Colonel Yorke, at the beginning of May 1898; there was an opening ceremony on the 11th when Lady Newnes cut coloured ribbons stretched across the track before the special train entered Lynton station. On Monday 16 May public traffic began.

Useful revenue was expected from the carriage of coal, which hitherto had been discharged by coasters on the beach at Lynmouth whence it had to be hauled *up* the hill to Lynton, but once the railway had completed a branch to a wharf beside the River Yeo at Barnstaple, coal could be carried by rail direct from the ship's side, carted *down* the hill, and sold in Lynton at far lower prices. This expectation was realised: mineral traffic averaged 2,908 tons a year from 1902 to 1913, and during the same period general merchandise, most of which flowed in the same direction, averaged 4,793 tons a year. But the two together indicate an average of no more than 25 tons per day, not enough to justify the running of separate goods trains; one was indeed scheduled to run 'when required' in the summer of 1924, but it was seldom needed as the traffic could easily be handled by attaching wagons to the passenger trains.

Inevitably, the Lynton & Barnstaple was essentially a passenger line,

Barnstaple Town station in early days. Staff posed alongside a mixed train, the London & South Western Railway station-master in command, and the railway dog probably with a collecting box for contributions to a railway orphanage. (*Kingsway Real Photo Series.*)

carrying an average of 96,989 a year between 1902 and 1913. As time had to be allowed for attaching or detaching wagons at the intermediate stations, overall speed was low, and the five trains put on in the summer of 1898 averaged 102 minutes in each direction for the journey of 19¼ miles. Although this was a considerable improvement over the speed of the horse-drawn coaches, it has to be remembered that passengers took some time to get to and from the stations, especially those at Blackmoor, Woody Bay and Lynton, all of which were far from the settlements they were intended to serve. Visitors, tourists and trippers benefited most. For many years in the early 1900s, day trippers could have a splendid day out, some from South Wales travelling by paddle steamer to Ilfracombe, train to Barnstaple and Lynton, and then returning by horse-drawn coach to Ilfracombe, or perhaps going forward by the coach which ran from Lynmouth through Porlock to Minehead, where they could board another steamer for home. Summer visitors used the railway for holidays in Lynton or Simonsbath or, as my parents and I did in 1927, to reach the Staghunters Inn at Brendon. Some holiday-makers staying in the locality made the journey for the sake of travelling over an intriguing little line, for in England, as distinct from Wales, there were never many narrow gauge

Chelfham Viaduct: eight brick spans of 42ft. each across the Stoke Rivers valley, with a maximum

Bratton Fleming, a picturesque spot and one of the two stations built by the contractor without a station house. A siding intersected the platform because of the limited space on the flank of the hillside. 11 August 1927.

Blackmoor station. As at Woody Bay and Lynton, the buildings were erected by the company in an attractive chalet style, but that at Blackmoor was larger as it included a refreshment room. This 1927 photograph shows the train from Lynton, headed by *Taw*, waiting while *Yeo* from Barnstaple draws into the loop.

passenger-carrying railways, and no others near the popular West Country holiday resorts; among those who did so in the later years were some who quitted their motor cars at one or other of the stations to ride on the train, presaging those present-day tourists who sustain the Ravenglass & Eskdale, Festiniog and Talyllyn Railways. All were entranced by the scenery which there was time to savour fully from the slow-moving trains, for Barnstaple–Lynton was a very beautiful ride.

The line began beside the River Taw, close to the mouth of the Yeo and the head of the Taw estuary. The London & South Western Railway built a new station, Barnstaple Town, with one platform, the outer face for its own trains on the single track to Ilfracombe, and a bay for the narrow gauge, for use of which the L & B Company paid rent. From the end of the bay platform the track rounded a sharp curve to bring it alongside the Yeo, the valley of which it followed for just on five miles. Crossing on the level two main roads on the edge of the town, the line passed Pilton Yard, the company's extensive depot where there were goods yard, engine and carriage sheds and repair shops, and headquarters offices. Beside the Yeo and the meadows, gradients were gentle, except for a half-mile bank at 1 in 55 where the line rose to cut across a loop of the river. But soon the valley narrowed, and hanging woods clad the opposite slope as the railway approached Snapper Halt, named after a nearby inn rather than the village of Goodleigh which lay a full three-quarters of a mile away as the crow flies and a good deal further by passengers' footsteps. Confined in the wooded valley with road and river, curves abounded and the climb along the flank of the hillside began, steepening to the 1 in 50 gradient that prevailed with little relief to the summit 12½ miles beyond. Approaching Chelfham station, there was a curved viaduct of eight brick arches, each 42ft. wide and with a maximum height of 70ft. above the Stoke Rivers combe, the major engineering work on the railway and said to have cost about £6,500.

Chelfham station was one of two built by the contractor with very simple accommodation, just a booking office and waiting room without a house for the station-master who had to live in the village. But it was very picturesque, for here as elsewhere there were well-tended flower beds, shrubs and climbing plants, encouraged by Sir George Newnes' offer of an annual prize of £5 for the best-kept station. In fact, it was not only at the stations that flowers flourished, as the Rev J. Chanter, Rector of Parracombe when the railway was built, had the charming habit of flinging seeds from the carriage window when he travelled!

A little north of Chelfham, the line quitted the Yeo and headed north-east up the Bratton valley and, clinging ever higher to its flank, reached Bratton Fleming, the second of the stations built by the contractor, and the only one really close to the village after which it was named. It was hoped that local slate would be railed here, so there were two sidings instead of just one serving a goods shed, but as the slate proved to be of poor quality, no such traffic developed. Beyond, the line turned up a side valley, passing through a rock cutting and rounding a horseshoe loop with a high embankment at its head pierced by culverts, one of which was an escape route for hunted Exmoor red deer, and two for hill streams flowing on either side of Southcott Farm. Within the next mile the track passed near the three farms named by Newbolt: Knightacott, Narracott and Hunnacott, with Sprecott (which now uses the abandoned track bed for its access road) between the last two. At Wistlandpound, there was another horseshoe bend, since drowned in a reservoir fed by three moorland streams. Trees gave place to bracken and gorse as the railway approached the watershed before reaching Blackmoor station for Blackmoor Gate, a hamlet with an inn at the crossroads of the Barnstaple–Lynton and South Molton–Combe Martin–Ilfracombe highways. Blackmoor, it was hoped, would be the most important wayside station, to which coaches would bring passengers from Ilfracombe to complete their journey to Lynton by rail. So there were stables for coach horses, a goods shed, a siding to each, and a refreshment room in the attractive station building, one of the three built by the company (after the failure of the contractor) in a distinctive chalet style with good accommodation for the station-master, part on the ground floor, part in the gable. But alas! it was a forlorn hope that passengers would relish changing to the train at Blackmoor when the coach they were on would take them into Lynton itself, and when Sir George Newnes tried to improve the service by substituting road motor buses in 1903, these were waylaid by the police who summonsed the drivers for travelling too fast on by-roads, and although it was claimed that the speed was little more than 8 mph, the magistrates inflicted severe fines and the buses were withdrawn.

Leaving Blackmoor, the line descended into a valley of northward-flowing streams feeding the River Heddon, crossing it by a horseshoe curve at the head of which the 1 in 50 climb began again. There were views north-westward towards Combe Martin and the Bristol Channel and, near at hand, of the village of Parracombe, three sides of which had indeed been in sight from any train rounding the horseshoe. Although Parracombe village was more conveniently served by its little Halt than most other communities along the route, passengers were so few at first that trains stopped there on Fridays only, market day in Barnstaple, and tickets were issued by the porter coming from Blackmoor. But within a year patronage increased sufficiently to justify a regular stop and to arrange for tickets to be available from the village post office – a strange proceeding perhaps, yet not so strange as at an Irish station I knew where the buildings on the platform housed booking office, post office and pub!

Away over the moorland commons for a mile and a half, the line reached Woody Bay station beside copses of firs in an empty landscape, almost at the summit. Great things were expected of the real Woody Bay three miles to the north and washed by the tides of the Bristol Channel; a hotel was built by 'developers' whose ambition was to create a new North Devon resort, and there was talk of serving it by a branch line and building a pier for paddle steamers to call at. But nothing came of this except the hotel and the name Woody Bay for the station at Martinhoe Cross, where the road running high over Martinhoe Common to Martinhoe village left the Barnstaple–Lynton highway.

There was another deep rock cutting before the railway began to thread the valley of the Barbrook at Outovercott hamlet – what a name, redolent of isolation! Descending at 1 in 50 and passing Caffyns Halt, the track rounded an elbow bend at Dean and a V-shaped loop high on the flank of the ravine above the confluence of the Barbrook and the West Lyn River. Thence it passed through woodland once again as it made its way to the Lynton terminus and the end of a fascinating journey.

Lynton station building was very similar to that at Blackmoor, with a refreshment room and accommodation for the station-master. Beyond the platform, which had a bay, was the goods shed and goods yard. There was of course a running round loop, and from this there was a spur to an engine shed as during the first season of operation a locomotive had to be stationed there to take the early morning train to Barnstaple.

Three 2–6–2 tank engines, *Yeo, Exe* and *Taw* (they bore no running numbers until included in Southern Railway stock), were built in 1897–8 by Manning Wardle & Co. at the Boyne Engine Works, Leeds, maker's numbers 1361–3, price £1,100 each. They were beautifully finished in a livery of dark green edged by a thin orange line and a wide black border, with outside frames and cylinders dark brown, chimney cap and dome of polished brass. Although Howey in 1935 referred to them contemptuously as 'dreadful old things with long funnels',★ most of those who paused to look at them before entraining at Barnstaple or Lynton felt that the good proportions, tasteful livery, immaculate condition and competent air of so small a machine exercised a certain charm. Their little driving wheels were only 2ft. 9in. diameter, and leading and trailing wheels 2ft. Weight was 27¼ tons. With 383 sq. ft. of heating surface, boiler pressure 160lb. per sq. in., and cylinders 10½in. × 16in., their tractive effort was 7,269lb.

After delivery, some minor alterations were made at Pilton. The safety valves had been placed within the cab, projecting upwards through the roof, but this led to wisps of steam collecting inside and misting the spectacle glasses, so roof and front of cab were moved back, enclosing the bunker which in any case was little used because coal stored on either side of the firebox forward of the cab was more easily reached by the fireman's shovel. The cylinders and motion had been totally enclosed, with an inspection cover which gave access to the valve gear, but in service it was found preferable to run without the cover plate and later to enlarge the opening.

It was soon realised that three locomotives would not be enough, as it was probable that in summer some trains would need a pilot engine, and of course allowance had to be made for regular washing out of boilers and sudden withdrawal for minor repairs. So even before the line was opened, it was decided to order a fourth. But Manning Wardle and other British firms

---

★   Snell, J.B., *One Man's Railway*, p. 62.

The curves at Barbrook on the descent to Lynton. From a card published by Frith & Co. and postmarked 13 July 1909.

Lynton terminus. The Baldwin *Lyn* was about to pull the train into the platform. The end of the bay platform can just be seen on the right, and behind the train is the goods shed. (*Peacock 'Autochrome' series.*)

Lyn with the ugly stove pipe chimney inflicted on her by Eastleigh Works. At Pilton, 11 August 1927.

Lew, built to order of the Southern Railway by Manning Wardle & Co. in 1925, using the original designs of 1897. At Pilton, 11 August 1927.

which specialised in building small engines were all fully occupied completing work which had been delayed by a strike of engineers. The order was therefore placed with the Baldwin Locomotive Works, Philadelphia, USA, which had no difficulty in designing and building a suitable engine quickly. The order was placed in February 1898, the locomotive was shipped in parts to England, and assembly was completed at Pilton in time for her to be steamed in July.

A 2–4–2 tank of typically American design with bar frames, a large cab, and two sand domes as well as a steam dome mounted on the boiler, *Lyn* had not the grace of the little Manning Wardles. A few alterations and adjustments had to be made, but she was sturdy and lasted out the life of the railway. Diameter of driving wheels was the same, of leading and trailing wheels 2in. less, cylinders half an inch less in diameter but with the same stroke, and heating surface less by 4 sq. ft., but as her boiler pressure was higher at 180lb., she had the greater tractive effort of 7,418lb. Yet her weight was only 22 tons. Baldwins delivered her painted black, relieved by a single yellow line, but they gave her chimney a neat copper cap. After a few years,

Brake Composite, L & B No. 15, SR 6993. Built at Bristol with two First Class and three Third Class compartments, as well as one for luggage and another, with duckets, for the guard. At Pilton, 11 August 1927.

she was repainted to match the other 'Rivers', and when her boiler was condemned in 1907 she received a new one built by the Avonside Engine Co. Unfortunately, during a visit to Eastleigh Works during the last years of the LSWR, *Lyn's* graceful Baldwin chimney was replaced by an exceptionally ugly stove pipe, and she was in that condition when I photographed her in August 1927.

The locomotive built to the order of the Southern Railway in 1925 came also from Manning Wardle, maker's number 2042, following the original designs with only minor alterations. The safety valves were forward of the cab, the redundant coal bunker was omitted, and the motion totally exposed with a drip tray beneath. She bore the name of another three-letter Devon river, *Lew*, a tributary of the Torridge which flows into the sea together with the Taw, west of Barnstaple. The Southern gave her its livery, a paler green lined in white and edged in black, frames black, SOUTHERN in bold yellow lettering on the side tanks above the name plate, and the number E 188 on the cab sides. In course of time, *Yeo, Exe, Taw* and *Lyn* appeared in similar guise, numbered E 759, 760, 761 and 762.

The Lynton & Barnstaple Company's passenger coaches were of interest because the directors were determined that tourists should be able to enjoy to the full the beauties of the ride. Hence, of the sixteen built by the Bristol Carriage & Wagon Works in 1897, varying in cost from £394 14*s*. 6*s*. to £527 18*s*. 6*d*., half included observation saloons with sides open above the waist; four had these compartments at the rear end and were for First Class passengers only; the other four, Third Class, had them in the middle. All eight had canvas blinds to exclude rain, but as these also excluded the view, they were removed after some five years and – First Class only! – replaced by sliding windows. The remaining eight coaches comprised four Thirds, two Composites and two Third brakes. One other coach, a Brake Composite, appeared from Pilton Works in 1903, the body probably built by a Barnstaple joinery firm and the running gear supplied from Bristol. Twelve of the 17 weighed 8 tons 16 cwt., and the other five 9 tons. All were 39½ft. long and had the same type of frame mounted on bogies; they were fitted with vacuum brakes and well lit, at first by oil lamps and later by acetylene. But the enterprising use of roller bearings for the first time in Britain was not a success as the ends tapered in service, so that experiment had to be abandoned. First Class seating was upholstered, but Third Class passengers sat on seats of bare slatted wood, until the Southern fitted many with a cushion. The early livery was lined white above the waist and lake (or a reddish-brown) below and on the ends, but later a single overall colour, probably lake, was adopted. All in all, the coaches were well built and maintained, and the standard of accommodation excelled that of other narrow gauge railways in this country. There were complaints that the vehicles rolled, but what else could be expected with a width of over 6ft. on a gauge of 2ft.?

For freight traffic, fourteen four-wheeled vehicles, each able to carry 4 tons, were built by the Bristol firm in 1897, eight as open wagons (tare 2 tons 7¾ cwt.), six as vans (tare 2 tons 11¾ cwt.), but at the same time another four vehicles were mounted on bogies and, as these were so obviously better suited to the severe curves, bogies became the standard for all later freight stock. Of the four, each of which could carry 8 tons, two were open (tare 5 tons 5½ cwt.), the other two vans (tare 5 tons 18½ cwt.). The bogie vans were designed to carry a guard, for whom there was a veranda at one end from which he could operate a brake, and, as well as side doors, there was entry to the platform from the van body through a windowed partition so that he could maintain observation from under cover. After some ten years, however, the veranda was made more suitable by enclosing it and providing windows in the rear end and above the side doors. Another van, built at Pilton in 1908 or 1909, had a proper compartment for the guard with an end window and projecting duckets from which he could see along the side of his train.

Three more open wagons were added, one probably acquired from the bankrupt contractor, one built at Bristol in 1903 and one at Pilton in 1913; and there were two flat wagons (Bristol, 1902) for long loads such as timber, or bulky ones like hay. Freight stock livery was light grey, relieved by black metalwork and white lettering.

These twenty-four goods vehicles sufficed until the company was absorbed by the Southern, which added four open tilt wagons (with a bar to support a tarpaulin) and four vans, all with the same capacity of 8 tons as had the previous bogie wagons, but of stronger construction and greater tare weight (6 tons 1 cwt. and 6 tons 6 cwt. respectively). These, lettered SR and painted in the standard SR goods livery of dark brown (or umber) inherited from the LSWR, were in course of delivery from J. & F. Howard Ltd. of Bedford at the date of my visit on 11 August 1927. Two second-hand breakdown cranes, able to lift a maximum weight of 4½ tons and probably originally built for the 60cm. gauge War Department railways, were bought in 1926 (a Match Truck to run with them was constructed by the SR at Lancing Works in 1927), but they were not really necessary as the rolling stock was light enough to be re-railed more simply by using jacks and timber baulks, so one became a mobile yard crane at Lynton and the other languished at Pilton. Like the passenger coaches, all but two of the wagons

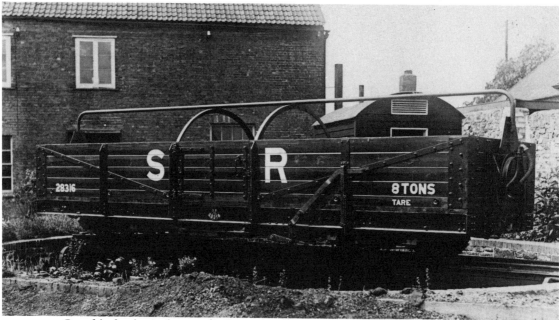

One of the four bogie tilt wagons built to order of the Southern Railway by J & F Howard Ltd. of Bedford in 1927. No. 28316 on the turntable at Pilton on 11 August 1927.

Of the four bogie vans built by Howard in 1927, three are seen here on delivery to Barnstaple, 11 August 1927. Nos. 47044 and 47045 were already railed on the narrow gauge track at the transhipment sidings and No. 47043 was about to be unloaded.

were fully fitted for vacuum brake operation in mixed trains, and the odd two were piped. Centre buffer-couplings of the type used by Norwegian narrow gauge railways, with a projecting hook like a formidable chopper, were fitted to all stock.

The first timetable, for the summer of 1898, shows a service of five trains each way on weekdays and one on Sundays; the earliest left Lynton at 6.14 a.m. and crossed the 6.35 from Barnstaple at Bratton, hence the need for an engine to be stabled overnight at Lynton. In general, three each way sufficed for winter working, with one extra on Fridays, market day in Barnstaple. In later years, this service increased to five in the early part of the summer season and to six at its height. Winter and summer, the first, leaving Barnstaple at 6.20 a.m., brought the newspapers and Royal Mail, fulfilling that valuable service which all the small railways gave to previously isolated country districts, and earning the small but steady income from the Post Office which was a useful contribution to the expense of running the off-season services. Nevertheless, the Mail included goods wagons if necessary and its timing was therefore little different from that of any other. In the summer of 1924, there were no less than seven regular passenger trains and one extra from Barnstaple on Fridays and Saturdays, a service which involved every one, except the morning Mail and the last from Lynton, crossing another, sometimes two others, en route, and use of the crossing loops at each of the four intermediate stations. Trains from Lynton, aided by the gradients, were quicker by a few minutes than those in the opposite direction, but otherwise individual timings varied little on either side of the average, which was gradually reduced over the years: 102.4 minutes in 1898, 87.4 in 1908, 84.2 in 1923, 81.4 in 1924, falling back to 89.6 in the summer of 1935, the last. But although the road motors of the 1930s took longer, 98 minutes for the shorter distance of 16 miles, bus passengers were saved the time and stress of the walks to and from the railway stations.

Traffic control was effective. Times in the Working Timetable were marked by an 'X' to show where trains would cross. Distant signals were not provided, but Home and Starting signals, interlocked with the points, controlled entry and exit at the passing loops and terminal stations. The six single-track sections between them were each protected by a pair of Tyer's Electric Tablet Instruments (rather like glorified cigarette slot machines), one at each end, electrically locked so that no second tablet could be extracted from either instrument until the first had been re-inserted; these were installed at Barnstaple Town, Pilton Bridge, Chelfham, Bratton Fleming, Blackmoor, Woody Bay and Lynton.

Barnstaple Town station was staffed by the London & South Western

Railway, but the Lynton & Barnstaple provided a signalman at its box and a goods porter at the transhipment sidings. There was also a manned signal box at Pilton, which controlled the points leading to and from the Yard and the signals on the running line, as well as locks on the gates of the two level crossings where there were crossing-keepers who opened and closed the gates by hand. At Lynton, the station-master had a man in charge of the goods yard, one platform porter all the year round and two in summer. At Blackmoor, the station-master always had the help of a porter, at Woody Bay, of one in summer only. But two stations were attended by one man alone, a porter-signalman at Chelfham, a station-master at Bratton Fleming. It was therefore essential that the tablet instruments at all four intermediate stations could be quickly reached from the platform to avoid delay to trains, so they were placed in the booking office. Even so, in summer when traffic was heavy, the porter-signalman at Chelfham would have been hard pressed, especially when two trains crossed there, as he had to set points and signals, exchange the tablets and attend to platform duties; and even harder pressed would have been the lone station-master at Bratton Fleming, for his was a busier station where there were more tickets to issue and collect and more parcels and passengers' luggage to handle.

The regular staff employed by the company probably numbered less than sixty, of whom three-quarters worked at, or were based at, Pilton: in the headquarters office were the General Manager and three clerks; two men, a clerk and a porter, managed the goods yard; the locomotive, carriage and wagon repair shops, supervised by a foreman, employed nine, among whom were a smith, a carpenter, two apprentices and two painters; the track was maintained by about sixteen platelayers under the direction of an inspector; there was a Signal & Telegraph linesman; and to run the trains, there were three regular drivers, firemen and guards, augmented by one more of each in summer.

Extra porters would no doubt have been found locally; the permanent way gang may have been increased by unskilled labourers; but a train crew cannot be recruited from the hedgerows, especially a driver who must know his machine and have been trained in knowledge of the route and operating methods, so it is likely that he and his fireman were drawn from the staff manning the workshops. All small railways undertake as much overhaul and heavy repair of locomotives and rolling stock as possible during the winter months when traffic is light, so that equipment will be available for the extra summer services and some workshop staff released for other duties.

Rehabilitation of the Lynton & Barnstaple was but a small part of the enterprise shown by the Southern Railway under Sir Herbert Walker's leadership during the second half of the 1920s. The major events were the spread of suburban electrification from 1925 onwards, the introduction the same year of the 'King Arthur' class engines to haul the expresses to Dover, Bournemouth and Exeter (later also to Brighton) and the appearance on these trains of R.E.L. Maunsell's coaches fitted with Third Class seating more comfortable than to be found elsewhere, and the buckeye couplings and wide Pullman-type gangways until then standard only on the LNER.

The principal North Devon and Cornwall express leaving Waterloo about 11 a.m. received this rolling stock in 1927 and was named the 'Atlantic Coast Express'. I determined to make my journey to Barnstaple on Saturday, 6 August by this train, although it involved joining a crowded Up Scottish express leaving York about 3.30 a.m. Kings Cross station had a barber's saloon where I was shaved, and of course a dining room where I was served an excellent and very welcome breakfast.

It is easy to say that the Southern ought never to have closed the picturesque Lynton & Barnstaple line in 1935 after spending so much on its improvement, but it cannot be denied that both passenger and goods traffic was far more conveniently served by road motor vehicles. Although under the old company, the railway had paid its way, it had never been prosperous, and only from 1913 to 1921 had any dividend been paid on the £84,976 in ordinary shares, and then only ½ per cent each year. Even before the Grouping of 1923, the company had sought relief from its strained financial position by negotiating terms for purchase by the LSWR, and eventually it became part of the Southern on 1 July 1923 for £39,267. The LSWR had lent £20,000 in 1905, secured by an issue of debentures, and as the loan was cancelled, it became possible to pay 70 per cent to other first debenture holders, 65 per cent to holders of the second debentures, and 6 per cent to shareholders. However, the Southern soon found that it lost between £5,000 and £6,000 a year by maintaining the line in operation.

Railway preservation had then no popular appeal, and it was not until sixteen years later that interest was awakened and men, and women also, came forward to form those working parties of volunteers whose enthusiasm and unpaid labour have made possible the preservation of many narrow gauge railways and branch lines.

So the last train left Lynton in the evening of Sunday, 29 September 1935, filled to capacity by nostalgic travellers and drawn by *Yeo* and *Lew*, the oldest and the newest of the engines. The excellent station buildings were sold by private treaty and found ready buyers at bargain prices, £700 for the best of them, that at Blackmoor, but a mass of equipment was sold by auction at Pilton on 13 November. The turntable was bought by Howey and installed at New Romney. *Lew* was acquired for £52 and shipped to Brazil for use on a coffee plantation, accompanied by steel frames of bogie stock, the wooden bodies of which were burnt. The other locomotives were cut up by a scrap merchant.

The coach I had photographed at Pilton in 1927 (L & B No. 15, SR 6993) somehow became marooned on an isolated length of rail at Snapper when track was lifted, and after many years in use as a hen house was bought for the Festiniog Railway in 1959, restored and put into service, bearing for a time the appropriate name of *The Snapper Bar* but re-named *William Madocks* later. Another, also marooned there, one of those with a First Class observation end (L & B No. 2, SR 6992), became a summer house in the garden of a Devon rectory until acquired in 1982 by the National Railway Museum.

What a pity that coach is not accompanied by one of the Manning Wardle engines! In 1935, the Southern could have presented one, as they did some of the nameplates, to the LNER Museum in York.

BIBLIOGRAPHY

Bowtell, Harold D. 'Railways in Colsterdale', *Journal of the Stephenson Locomotive Society*, Vol 40, May 1964, pp. 143–153.

Boyd, J.I.C. *Narrow Gauge Rails in Mid-Wales*, pp. 81–90.
The Fairbourne Miniature Railway. Oakwood Press, 1952.

Brown, G.A., Prideaux, J.C.D.A. and Radcliffe, H.G. *The Lynton & Barnstaple Railway*. David & Charles, Newton Abbot, 1964, new edition 1971/1986.

Butterell, Robin. *Steam on Britain's Miniature Railways 7¼" to 15" gauge*. D. Bradford Barton, Truro, 1976.

Catchpole, L.T. *The Lynton & Barnstaple Railway*. Oakwood Press, 1936, sixth edition 1972/1983.

Clayton, H., Jacot, M. and Butterell, R. *Miniature Railways, Vol 1, 15 Inch*. Oakwood Press, no date, *c.*1970.

Davies, W.J.K. *The Ravenglass & Eskdale Railway*. David & Charles, Newton Abbot, 1968, second edition 1981.

Davies, W.J.K. *The Romney Hythe & Dymchurch Railway*. David & Charles, Newton Abbot, 1975.

Greenly, Henry. *The Ravenglass & Eskdale Narrow Gauge (15") Railway, The Smallest Railway in the World*. Ravenglass & Eskdale Railway, 1923, reprinted 1987.

Hartley, Ken. *The Sand Hutton Light Railway*. Narrow Gauge Railway Society, 1964, second edition revised and enlarged 1982.

Heywood, Sir Arthur Percival, Bt. *Minimum Gauge Railways, their application, construction and working*. Privately published third edition 1898, typewritten reproduction of text produced by C.R. Clinker, 1950.

Household, H.G.W. 'The Sand Hutton Light Railway', *Locomotive Railway Carriage & Wagon Review*, Vol 34, 1928, pp. 326–9.

Jenner, David, and van Zeller, Peter. *The R & ER Stockbook*. Ravenglass & Eskdale Preservation Society Ltd., 1988.

Mosley, David, and van Zeller, Peter. *Fifteen Inch Gauge Railways, their history, equipment and operation.* David & Charles, Newton Abbot, 1986.

Railway Magazine, Vol 34, 1914, pp. 229–36, 'The Sand Hutton Railway', by Voyageur. (The 15-inch gauge line); Vol 36, 1915, pp. 59–62, 'A Remarkable Miniature Locomotive', by Voyageur. (The testing of *John Anthony* at Eaton Hall); Vol 115, 1969, p. 435–8, 'Back to Square One', by A.N. Mackay. (The Harrogate Gas Works Railway); Vol 123, 1977, pp. 84–8, 'Cavalcade in Miniature', by Robin Butterell. (The narrow gauge gathering at Ravenglass); Vol 125, 1979, pp. 262–5, 'Rebuilding Romney Rail', by J.B. Snell; Vol 126, 1980, p. 538, 'Eskdale's "First Lady"'; Vol 127, 1981, pp. 136–9, 'Narrow Gauge to Lynton', by Christopher B. Wesson; Vol 132, 1986, pp. 546–50, 'Locomotive Exchanges on the 15 inch Gauge', by Peter van Zeller.

Railway World Special: The Romney Hythe & Dymchurch Railway. Ian Allan, Shepperton, 1985.

Robertson, Leslie S. *Narrow Gauge Railways, Two Feet and Under.* A treatise first published in 1898, new edition with additional material and a new introduction by Andrew Neale, Plateway Press, Croydon, 1988.

Snell, J.B. *One Man's Railway, J.E.P. Howey and The Romney Hythe & Dymchurch Railway.* David & Charles, Newton Abbot, 1983.

Townsley, D.H. 'One for the Mud, A Hunslet contribution to trench warfare which later did International Service', *Model Railways*, 1976. (Describes adaptation of a Hunslet locomotive for Harrogate Gas Works).

Walker, Sir Robert J.M. Bt. 'Light Railways and Agriculture', *Railway Magazine*, Vol 54, 1924, pp. 361–7.

'The Sand Hutton Light Railway', *Railway Magazine*, Vol 55, 1924, pp. 432–7.

Whitehead, R.A. 'Miniature Railways', *Locomotive Railway Carriage & Wagon Review*, Vol 48, 1942, pp. 14–17, 50–4, 96–8, 128–30, 159–61, 193–4.